Key Drivers of Environmental Innovation

Hidemichi Fujii

Key Drivers of Environmental Innovation

Patent Data Analysis for R&D Policy Making toward Green Transformation

Springer

Hidemichi Fujii
Faculty of Economics
Kyushu University
Fukuoka, Japan

ISBN 978-981-92-0059-7 ISBN 978-981-92-0060-3 (eBook)
https://doi.org/10.1007/978-981-92-0060-3

This Springer imprint is published by the registered company Springer Nature Singapore Pte Ltd.
The registered company address is: 152 Beach Road, #21-01/04 Gateway East, Singapore 189721, Singapore

Preface

Achieving sustainable development is one of the most challenging and urgent tasks facing modern society. Addressing environmental issues such as climate change, air pollution, and water pollution is no longer merely an ethical imperative; it has become an essential investment to ensure economic sustainability. Against this backdrop, strategic initiatives aimed at creating and socially implementing innovative environmental technologies are accelerating worldwide.

This book aims to elucidate the reality of R&D strategies in key environmental technology fields from an environmental economics perspective, using objective and quantitative patent data as the primary indicator. Specifically, it focuses on three critical domains: renewable energy (Chap. 3), environmentally friendly vehicles (Chap. 4), and pollution control technologies (Chap. 5).

The core of the analysis is a patent factor decomposition analysis using the logarithmic mean Divisia index (LMDI), detailed in Chap. 2. This methodology enables the analysis of multifaceted factors—beyond mere patent volume fluctuations—such as the underlying "scale of R&D (SCALE)," "overall intensity of focus on environmental technologies (ENVIRONMENT)," and "strategic prioritization of specific technologies (PRIORITY)."

Through this book, readers will gain an understanding of the dynamics of environmental technological innovation across the IP5 patent offices—the Japan Patent Office (JPO), China National Intellectual Property Administration (CNIPA), United States Patent and Trademark Office (USPTO), European Patent Office (EPO), and Korean Intellectual Property Office (KIPO) within a data-backed theoretical framework. I sincerely hope this book serves as a compass for policymakers, corporate technology strategists, and researchers aspiring to pursue environmental economics, guiding them as they take their next steps.

Fukuoka, Japan

Hidemichi Fujii

Acknowledgements The research results included in this book were carried out with substantial support from the Japan Society for the Promotion of Science (JSPS) Grant-in-Aid for Scientific Research (B) [25K03328]. I hereby express my deepest gratitude.

Contents

Chapter 1
Introduction

1.1 Background and Importance of Environmental Technologies

The effective and economic control of environmental pollution with limited budgets and labor resources is essential for sustainable development. Environmental conservation technologies (environmental technologies) play an important role in efforts to achieve sustainable development, and the research and development of environmental technologies is advancing worldwide.

Recent systematic reviews have shown that environmental regulation continues to be a major driver of green technology innovation across nations, although the effects vary based on regulatory approaches and technological contexts (Borsatto & Bazani, 2021; Zhang et al., 2024). In Japan, the "Innovative Environmental Innovation Strategy" was formulated based on the "Long-term Strategy under the Paris Agreement as Growth Strategy" and the "Integrated Innovation Strategy 2019," which were approved by the Cabinet in June 2019. This strategy aims to achieve significant greenhouse gas reductions through the creation of innovative technologies and cost reductions for social implementation.

Additionally, Europe has formulated the "European Green Deal Strategy" to promote technological development aimed at solving various environmental problems, including climate change and marine plastic pollution. More recently, the European Union introduced the Fit for 55 package in 2021 and the Net Zero Industry Act in 2023, further strengthening its commitment to environmental technology innovation and deployment.

These policies commonly have two aspects: economic policies to recover from economic downturns associated with the COVID-19 pandemic and science and technology policies aimed at addressing worsening climate change issues. These policies can be characterized as technology development strategies that combine economic recovery with climate change measures. This dual approach has become increasingly important in recent years, as Hötte and Jee (2022) have demonstrated that

H. Fujii, *Key Drivers of Environmental Innovation*,
https://doi.org/10.1007/978-981-92-0060-3_1

knowledge development for climate change adaptation technologies has accelerated substantially, with patent activity showing distinct geographical and technological clustering patterns that reflect both environmental concerns and economic priorities.

While I simply describe these technologies as environmental technologies, their targets cover a wide range, and the pollutants to be addressed include greenhouse gases, toxic chemicals, and dust/soot, among others. Furthermore, the motivations for developing environmental technologies are diverse and include pollution control (e.g., treating exhaust gases, industrial wastewater, and waste), energy-savings (e.g., reducing energy consumption), and reduction of environmental impact when end-users use products by improvements in the environmental performance of the products. Jin et al. (2019) have shown that technological innovation in industrial water resource management has significant positive effects on green total factor efficiency, highlighting the importance of precision in how I categorize and evaluate different environmental technologies.

Let us consider the costs and benefits of technological development for each situation. Research and development of environmental technologies aimed at reducing a company's own pollution is an additional investment in nonproduction sectors and does not directly lead to revenue; thus, the motivation for technology development for pollution prevention technologies cannot be considered high. On the contrary, in product design technology development, improving the energy efficiency of products (for example, improving automobile fuel efficiency) is expected to enhance product competitiveness; thus, companies have a high motivation to advance technology development. As such, differences in where environmental technologies are introduced and the economic benefits when they are introduced are believed to have a significant impact on technology development strategies.

Recent research by Chen et al. (2017) on agricultural pollution regulation demonstrates how targeted subsidies can effectively incentivize cleaner production technologies despite initial cost considerations, offering important lessons for other sectors. Research on decision-making related to the development of environmental technologies has accumulated, primarily in the United States and Europe, where patent databases were established early. Studies targeting the United States include the work of Brunnermeier and Cohen (2003), who analyzed the causal relationship between the number of environmental technology patents acquired, pollution control costs, and the number of government monitoring inspections in the manufacturing industry, and that of Carrión-Flores and Innes (2010), who analyzed the relationship between the number of environmental technology patents and chemical emissions, focusing on chemicals regulated under the U.S. Clean Air Act.

Additionally, as mentioned earlier, environmental technology research and development strategies differ because of differences in technological characteristics; thus, research has been conducted on individual technology fields to account for these differences. Research in this area includes that by Albino et al. (2014), who focused on the development of low-carbon technologies in the United States, and that by Barbieri (2015), who focused on the research and development of low-emission vehicle technologies in Europe.

Many existing studies on environmental technologies have focused on technology development, while research focusing on technology diffusion and implementation has been limited. One reason for this difference is the scarcity of objective and quantitative methods for evaluating technology diffusion and implementation. However, Grafström and Lindman (2017) have recently made significant contributions in this area by examining the entire innovation chain—from invention through innovation to diffusion—in the European wind power sector, providing valuable methodologies that can be applied to other environmental technologies.

Table 1.1 shows a comparison of environmental technology evaluation methods by stage of development, diffusion, and implementation, as presented by Haščič and Migotto (2015). As shown in Table 1.1, many methods are introduced to evaluate technology development, and the quantitative data used to evaluate the degree of technology development are relatively easy to obtain.

Among these data, the number of patents obtained holds significant strengths for evaluating technological development. All patents are systematically classified using the International Patent Classification and are publicly disclosed by each patent office. Furthermore, because patents also provide citation information, understanding the mechanisms of technology diffusion through citation networks becomes possible. The theoretical foundation for using patent data as an economic indicator was established by Griliches (1990), who systematically examined the relationship between patents and R&D activity. Griliches (1990) demonstrated that patent counts, despite their limitations, serve as a useful proxy variable for the output of R&D investment, reflecting the inventive activity of firms and industries. This framework has since provided the methodological basis for a wide range of studies analyzing technological development across sectors, including the environmental technology research examined in this chapter.

In contrast, data for evaluating technology diffusion and implementation, such as patent licensing fees and market penetration rates, are often classified as confidential company information, making data acquisition difficult. Furthermore, with respect to international trade transaction volumes using government statistics, it is difficult to obtain detailed data byproduct, which limits the ability to evaluate the degree of diffusion for specific technologies (for example, while the transaction volume of automobiles as a whole can be obtained, it is difficult to obtain transaction volumes by performance levels for exhaust gas control or fuel efficiency).

Against this backdrop, research on environmental technologies tends to focus on technology development utilizing patent information. With recent advances in artificial intelligence and computer processing power, analytical methods leveraging machine learning and natural language processing have evolved. These analytical advancements enhance the potential of patent data analysis, thereby advancing the understanding of the mechanisms governing the development, diffusion, and implementation of environmental technologies.

Table 1.1 Comparison of evaluation methods by technology development stage

Evaluation target	Evaluation items	Advantages (+) and Disadvantages (−)
Technology development	R&D expenditure and number of researchers	(+) Can examine the degree of resource input aimed at technology development (−) Input factor for technology development, not output factor (−) Difficult to evaluate only the development of environmental technologies (−) Difficult to obtain data except in advanced countries and limited industries
	Number of academic papers published	(+) Can be obtained from search functions in databases (+) Can analyze the importance of literature from citation data (−) The method of setting search keywords greatly influences the results (−) Need to verify how search keywords are used in the context of the paper
	Number of patent publications	(+) Can be regarded as an output factor of R&D (+) Environmental technologies can be identified using patent classifications (+) Can analyze importance using patent citation data (+) Data can be easily obtained from free databases (−) Cannot grasp the latest R&D status due to the existence of patent examination periods
Technology diffusion & implementation	Number of patent publications	(+) Patent acquisition status in foreign applications can be easily understood (−) Only evaluates patent technology, cannot evaluate product diffusion
	International trade transaction volume	(−) Difficult to identify products related to environmental protection technologies (−) Detailed data are often company confidential and difficult to obtain

(continued)

Table 1.1 (continued)

Evaluation target	Evaluation items	Advantages (+) and Disadvantages (−)
	License fees	(+) Can be used as a proxy variable for the degree of environmental technology implementation (−) Detailed data are often company confidential and difficult to obtain
	Sales of environmental protection equipment and market penetration	(+) Can be used as a proxy variable for the degree of implementation of environmental protection equipment (−) Detailed data are often company confidential and difficult to obtain

Source Created by the author based on Haščič and Migotto (2015) and Fujii and Managi (2017a), with partial modifications and supplementation

1.2 Literature Review: Research Focusing on Environmental Technology Development

Research focusing on environmental technology development often highlights the elements that promote research and development. Many of these studies apply econometric approaches to analyze how explanatory variables, which are causal variables, affect dependent variables, which are result variables.

In analytical models, the number of patents obtained is often used as the dependent variable, with research and development expenditure and variables related to environmental and energy policies as explanatory variables. By investigating patterns of technological specialization in green technologies across different countries, Corrocher and Solito (2022) recently expanded this approach and found significant heterogeneity in specialization patterns that reflects differing national innovation systems and policy priorities. This approach has been further refined in recent research by Du et al. (2019), who demonstrated that while green technology innovations generally contribute to carbon dioxide emission reduction, the effectiveness varies significantly by technology type and implementation context, thus highlighting the importance of targeted development strategies.

There are two ways to set the dependent variable: the number of patents and the percentage of all patents. In the latter case, it is possible to explicitly consider how much priority is given to technology development in a specific field compared to other fields, and this information is often used in analyses focusing on research and development strategies.

In Popp (2002), a representative study focusing on environmental technology development, the percentage of energy-related patents of the total number of patents obtained is used as the dependent variable, revealing the influence of intellectual resources, energy prices, and subsidies from the U.S. government. Johnstone et al. (2010) and Lanzi et al. (2012) conducted analyses using the number of patent applications and claims for energy-related technologies as dependent variables. The analysis method applies a negative binomial regression model, which is often used when the dependent variable is count data with a large variance. Because patent information is often used in analyses such as count data, counting how many patents have been filed or obtained, studies using count data as the dependent variable tend to apply negative binomial regression models.

Next, I introduce the work of Haščič and Migotto (2015), who focused on patent technologies developed through multinational collaborative research by examining the nationality data of patent applicants and analyzed their characteristics. This study collected patent information from the patent database PATSTAT, which was constructed and published by the European Patent Office (EPO), and compared the international collaboration intensity in research and development by technology classification by classifying technologies using the International Patent Classification (IPC) assigned to each patent.

The supplementary material of Haščič and Migotto (2015) contains a correspondence table for environmental technology classifications, which can be used to identify patents related to environmental technologies based on IPC. IPC mapping can be performed using general spreadsheet software. Barbieri et al. (2020) extended this work by examining how knowledge sources affect the impact of green versus nongreen technologies on subsequent inventions. Their findings reveal that compared with nongreen technologies, green technologies draw on more scientific sources and have a broader impact across technological domains, suggesting important implications for knowledge diffusion patterns in environmental innovation.

Finally, I introduce research that has analyzed changes in patent application strategies. By applying a factor decomposition analysis method called the log mean Divisia index (LMDI) to the number of patent applications, it is possible to decompose changes in the number of patent applications for specific technologies into changes in technology development strategy and in the research and development scale.

Studies that have applied factor decomposition analysis to the number of patent applications include Fujii and Managi (2016), who focused on environmental technologies in Japan; Fujii (2016), who analyzed green chemical technology inventions; Fujii and Managi (2019), who focused on environmental technologies in China; Fujii and Managi (2017b), who focused on industrial wastewater treatment technologies worldwide; and Fujii and Managi (2018), who investigated global trends in artificial intelligence technology. This methodology has proven particularly valuable for understanding how national innovation systems respond to changing environmental priorities and market conditions.

1.3 Literature Review: Research Focusing on Environmental Technology Diffusion

Next, I introduce research focusing on the diffusion of environmental technologies. As mentioned in Sect. 1.2, methods and data for quantitatively evaluating technology diffusion are limited, but within these constraints, studies focusing on environmental technology diffusion have been reported using patent citation information and author data from academic papers.

An important recent contribution in this area comes from Zhang and Gallagher (2020), who demonstrated that innovation and technology transfer through global value chains have been crucial to the development of China's photovoltaic industry, highlighting how industry-specific dynamics can accelerate environmental technology diffusion across borders. Popp (2006) analyzed how the strength of environmental regulations in the United States, Japan, and Germany affected the diffusion of emission control technologies for sulfur dioxide (SO_2) and nitrogen oxides (NO_x). The data used are patent acquisition data and patent citation numbers, and SO_2 and NO_x emission control technology patents are identified using IPC. In this study, the number of patent citations is used to evaluate the degree of technology diffusion, and an econometric model with the number of patent citations as the dependent variable is used to reveal the impact of strengthening environmental regulations on the degree of technology diffusion.

Dechezleprêtre et al. (2015) evaluated the degree of technology diffusion using combinations of patent registration countries and the location of technology developers. The analysis targets automobile emission standards, quantifies standard values and uses the differences in regulatory intensity between countries as explanatory variables for technology diffusion. While existing studies have focused mainly on domestic environmental regulations, this study is highly novel in considering the differences in regulatory levels between countries, which are important for technology diffusion.

Many of the studies introduced so far have been conducted using patent databases such as the World Intellectual Property Organization's (WIPO) Patentscope and the EPO's PATSTAT. In addition to the construction of large-scale patent databases, the spread of the internet has made it possible to obtain patent information online, making it easy to collect the patent information necessary to apply the analytical frameworks proposed by Popp (2006) and Dechezleprêtre et al. (2015).

In this context, the analytical framework that evaluates the degree of technology diffusion from the relationship between the location of the patent developer (company) and the registration country is expected to become a representative approach in the study of the degree of technology diffusion.

Recent work by Ardito et al. (2021) on technological convergence and open innovation has expanded the understanding of how knowledge production paradigms are shifting toward innovative ecosystems. Their research emphasizes the importance of collaborative approaches to advancing environmental technology, particularly as solutions to complex environmental challenges require the integration of knowledge from diverse fields.

The field of patent analysis within environmental technology has experienced substantial methodological advancements in recent years. The incorporation of artificial intelligence and machine learning techniques has facilitated increasingly sophisticated approaches to patent text analysis, enabling the identification of innovation patterns that remained largely obscured through conventional analytical frameworks. Hötte and Jee (2022) have documented substantial acceleration in knowledge development for adaptation technologies, with patent activity showing distinct geographical clustering that reflects regional vulnerability to climate impacts. This geographical specialization pattern suggests that local environmental challenges are increasingly driving targeted innovation efforts.

1.4 Objective and Contribution of This Book

This chapter focused on evaluation methods for environmental technologies using patent information, introduced previous studies on each stage of technology development and diffusion, and explained analytical methods using concrete examples that readers can refer to when conducting their own analyses.

Environmental technologies play important roles in implementing effective and economic pollution control and are essential elements in achieving sustainable development. While environmental technology development has largely been led by developed countries, it is becoming difficult to allocate ample budgets to policies and systems for the research, development, and diffusion of environmental technologies as was done in the past, amid the expansion of social security-related budgets in these countries.

Given this background, to promote the development and diffusion of environmental technologies under strict budget constraints, it is necessary to identify the factors influencing technology development from past data and to formulate science-based policies based on their causal relationships. The utilization of patent information is essential for achieving these research goals.

In advancing research that focuses on specific environmental technologies, identifying the technological classification of each patent is necessary. Environmental technology classification tables are introduced in Haščič and Migotto (2015), as mentioned in Sect. 1.2, as well as in WIPO's IPC green inventory. Additionally, classification tables for biotechnology and genetic resource-related technologies are published in Oldham (2004), and analyses of patent application numbers using this technology classification have been conducted in Fujii et al. (2016).

These technology classifications publish technology classification correspondence tables based on IPC, making it possible to easily classify technologies by using them in conjunction with patent databases. Recent improvements in patent databases have enabled researchers to construct environmental technology patent datasets more efficiently. Furthermore, technology classification correspondence tables using IPC have been reported in various technology fields, such as environmental technologies and biological technologies.

These trends support research activities targeting environmental technologies, and further development of research on environmental technologies utilizing patent information can be expected in the future. With respect to the future of environmental technology innovation research, the work of Hötte and Jee (2022) on climate change adaptation technologies and the integrated approaches to technological innovation systems outlined by Grafström and Lindman (2017) provide promising new methodological frameworks.

The subsequent chapters examine changes in environmental technology research strategies through detailed patent analysis. Each chapter focuses on a specific technology field and presents analyses of innovation trends, factors affecting patent invention strategy, and policy implications. This approach enables readers to gain both methodological knowledge of patent data analysis and a substantive understanding of how R&D strategies have shifted.

References

Albino, V., Ardito, L., Dangelico, R. M., & Petruzzelli, A. M. (2014). Understanding the development trends of low-carbon energy technologies: A patent analysis. *Applied Energy, 135,* 836–854.

Ardito, L., Petruzzelli, A. M., & Pascucci, F. (2021). Technological convergence, open innovation, and dynamic economy: Knowledge production paradigm shifts toward innovative ecosystem. *IEEE Transactions on Engineering Management, 68*(5), 1363–1380.

Barbieri, N. (2015). Investigating the impacts of technological position and European environmental regulation on green automotive patent activity. *Ecological Economics, 117,* 140–152.

Barbieri, N., Marzucchi, A., & Rizzo, U. (2020). Knowledge sources and impacts on subsequent inventions: Do green technologies differ from non-green ones? *Research Policy, 49*(2), Article 103901.

Borsatto, J. M. L. S., & Bazani, C. L. (2021). Green innovation and environmental regulations: A systematic review of international academic works. *Environmental Science and Pollution Research, 28*(45), 63751–63768.

Brunnermeier, S. B., & Cohen, M. A. (2003). Determinants of environmental innovation in US manufacturing industries. *Journal of Environmental Economics and Management, 45*(2), 278–293.

Carrión-Flores, C. E., & Innes, R. (2010). Environmental innovation and environmental performance. *Journal of Environmental Economics and Management, 59*(1), 27–42.

Chen, Y. H., Wen, X. W., Wang, B., & Nie, P. Y. (2017). Agricultural pollution and regulation: How to subsidize agriculture? *Journal of Cleaner Production, 164,* 258–264.

Corrocher, N., & Solito, I. (2022). Patterns of technological specialization in green technologies: Evidence from patent applications. *Industry and Innovation, 29*(3), 301–330.

Dechezleprêtre, A., Neumayer, E., & Perkins, R. (2015). Environmental regulation and the cross-border diffusion of new technology: Evidence from automobile patents. *Research Policy, 44*(1), 244–257.

Du, K., Li, P., & Yan, Z. (2019). Do green technology innovations contribute to carbon dioxide emission reduction? Empirical evidence from patent data. *Technological Forecasting and Social Change, 146,* 297–303.

Fujii, H. (2016). Decomposition analysis of green chemical technology inventions from 1971 to 2010 in Japan. *Journal of Cleaner Production, 112*(5), 4835–4843.

Fujii, H., & Managi, S. (2016). Research and development strategy for environmental technology in Japan: A comparative study of the private and public sectors. *Technological Forecasting & Social Change, 112,* 293–302.

Fujii, H., & Managi, S. (2017a). Evaluation of environmental protection technologies. In T. H. Arimura, H. Katayama, & S. Matsumoto (Eds.), *Frontiers of environmental economics* (pp. 3–17). Japan Hyoronsha.

Fujii, H., & Managi, S. (2017b). Decomposition analysis of water treatment technology patents. *Water, 9*(11), 860.

Fujii, H., & Managi, S. (2018). Trends and priority shifts in artificial intelligence technology invention: A global patent analysis. *Economic Analysis and Policy, 58,* 60–69.

Fujii, H., & Managi, S. (2019). Decomposition analysis of sustainable green technology inventions in China. *Technological Forecasting & Social Change, 139,* 10–16.

Fujii, H., Yoshida, K., & Sugimura, K. (2016). Research and development strategy in biological technologies: Patent data analysis in Japanese manufacturing firms. *Sustainability, 8*(4), 351.

Grafström, J., & Lindman, Å. (2017). Invention, innovation and diffusion in the European wind power sector. *Technological Forecasting and Social Change, 114,* 179–191.

Griliches, Z. (1990). Patent statistics as economic indicators: A survey. *Journal of Economic Literature, 28*(4), 1661–1707.

Haščič, I., & Migotto, M. (2015). *Measuring environmental innovation using patent data* (OECD Environment Working Papers No. 89). OECD Publishing.

Hötte, K., & Jee, S. J. (2022). Knowledge for a warmer world: A patent analysis of climate change adaptation technologies. *Technological Forecasting and Social Change, 183,* Article 121879.

Jin, W., Zhang, H. Q., Liu, S. S., & Zhang, H. B. (2019). Technological innovation, environmental regulation, and green total factor efficiency of industrial water resources. *Journal of Cleaner Production, 211,* 61–69.

Johnstone, N., Haščič, I., & Popp, D. (2010). Renewable energy policy and technological innovation: Evidence based on patent counts. *Environmental and Resource Economics, 45,* 133–155.

Lanzi, E., Haščič, I., & Johnstone, N. (2012). *The determinants of invention in electricity generation technologies: A patent data analysis* (OECD Environment Working Papers No. 45). OECD Publishing.

Oldham, P. (2004). Biodiversity and the patent system: Towards international indicators, global status and trends in intellectual property claims. *SSRN Electronic Journal,* (3).

Popp, D. (2002). Inducing innovation and energy prices. *The American Economic Review, 92*(1), 160–180.

Popp, D. (2006). International innovation and diffusion of air pollution control technologies: The effects of NO_x and SO_2 regulation in the US, Japan, and Germany. *Journal of Environmental Economics and Management, 51,* 46–71.

Zhang, F., & Gallagher, K. S. (2020). Innovation and technology transfer through global value chains: Evidence from China's PV industry. *Energy Policy, 147,* Article 111805.

Zhang, W., Zhu, B., Li, Y., & Yan, D. (2024). Revisiting the Porter hypothesis: A multi-country meta-analysis of the relationship between environmental regulation and green innovation. *Humanities and Social Sciences Communications, 11*(1), Article 232.

Chapter 2
Patent Decomposition Analysis

2.1 Introduction to Patent Decomposition Analysis

Patent data analysis is the process of analyzing patent documents and related information using statistical, informational, and business analysis methods. It is used to understand technological trends, evaluate competitive situations, formulate research and development strategies, and discover new markets by leveraging patent information. Patent data analysis serves as an essential tool for extracting insights into important technologies, market trends, and competitive landscapes by analyzing patent documents and the associated information (Griliches, 1990; Mejia & Kajikawa, 2024). The importance, necessity, and applications of patent data analysis are explained below.

Patent data analysis is key to understanding trends in specific technological fields or industries. Analysis of patent application numbers and citation relationships makes possible the identification of growing technologies and the prediction of future market directions. Patent data analysis is also essential for understanding competitors' technology portfolios and patent strategies. Through competitive analysis, companies can compare their technologies with those of competitors and formulate strategies to maintain or enhance competitiveness.

Patent data analysis is an indispensable tool for technological innovation and maintaining competitiveness and serves as a vital methodology to support strategic decision-making for companies and research institutions. Particularly in the knowledge economy era, the optimal utilization of knowledge assets is a source of competitiveness, and patent data analysis contributes to its realization (Nagaoka et al., 2010).

H. Fujii, *Key Drivers of Environmental Innovation*,
https://doi.org/10.1007/978-981-92-0060-3_2

2.2 Conceptual Framework and Indicators for Decomposition

In this section, I introduce an analytical method for examining the factors affecting the development of specific environmental technologies using patent information. Popp (2002) used the proportion of energy-related patents in total patent acquisitions as the dependent variable in research on energy-saving technology development. This allowed analysis of the effects of knowledge stock, energy prices, and government subsidies on the relative importance of R&D for energy-saving technologies. This approach demonstrated that patent shares effectively capture the relative priority given to specific technologies within firms' overall R&D portfolios. More recently, Gugler et al. (2024) extended this methodological framework by examining how environmental policies—including carbon taxes, environmental regulations, and R&D subsidies—direct technological change toward green innovation across multiple countries and industrial sectors. Their empirical analysis, using the share of green (Y02) patents as a key outcome measure, confirmed that patent shares serve as reliable indicators of strategic shifts in research priorities and resource allocation decisions.

To help readers visualize the explanation, I set up a dataset in Table 2.1 with three items: patent applications related to wind power technology (WIND), patent applications related to renewable energy technology (RENEWABLE), and total patent applications (TOTAL). This is a hypothetical example designed to illustrate how decomposition analysis works when scale decreases while priority increases. Note that wind power technology patent applications are included in renewable energy technology patent applications, and renewable energy technology patent applications are included in total patent applications.

The patent application data for Company A in 2020 and 2025 are shown in Table 2.1. Next, I explain two indicators necessary for the analysis. The first indicator is PRIORITY, which relates to the relative development priority of wind power technology within renewable energy technologies and is defined as $\frac{\text{PATENT}_{\text{WIND}}}{\text{PATENT}_{\text{RENEWABLE}}}$. An increase in this indicator means that research and development of wind power technology is being prioritized over other renewable energy technologies in Company A, as the proportion of wind power technology in renewable energy patent applications increases.

Table 2.1 Sample dataset for patent decomposition analysis (Unit: Number of Patents)

Year	Number of patents related to wind power technology ($\text{PATENT}_{\text{WIND}}$)	Number of patents related to renewable energy technology ($\text{PATENT}_{\text{RENEWABLE}}$)	Total number of technology patents ($\text{PATENT}_{\text{TOTAL}}$)
2020	10	50	500
2025	40	100	400

The second indicator is RENEWABLE, which indicates the proportion of renewable energy technology patent applications of total patent applications and thus reflects the development priority of renewable energy technology within overall research and development. Like the wind power technology priority indicator, the priority of renewable energy technology is defined as $\frac{\text{PATENT}_{\text{RENEWABLE}}}{\text{PATENT}_{\text{TOTAL}}}$. Finally, the SCALE indicator is defined as the total number of patents and thus represents the scale of national research and development (R&D) activity. It is affected by macro factors such as R&D policies and economic conditions.

Using these two indicators, the number of wind power technology patent applications can be expressed as Eq. (2.1):

$$\begin{aligned}\text{PATENT}_{\text{WIND}} &= \frac{\text{PATENT}_{\text{WIND}}}{\text{PATENT}_{\text{RENEWABLE}}} \times \frac{\text{PATENT}_{\text{RENEWABLE}}}{\text{PATENT}_{\text{TOTAL}}} \times \text{PATENT}_{\text{TOTAL}} \\ &= \text{PRIORITY} \times \text{RENEWABLE} \times \text{SCALE}\end{aligned}$$

Figure 2.1 visually illustrates the nested structure underlying this decomposition. Wind power technology patents ($\text{PATENT}_{\text{WIND}}$) form the innermost layer, contained within renewable energy technology patents ($\text{PATENT}_{\text{RENEWABLE}}$), which in turn are contained within total patent applications ($\text{PATENT}_{\text{TOTAL}}$). Each of the three indicators on the right side of the figure corresponds to one layer of this nested structure: SCALE reflects the outermost layer and captures the overall scale of R&D activity; RENEWABLE captures the relative priority of renewable energy technology within total patents; and PRIORITY captures the relative priority of wind power technology within renewable energy patents. This nested visualization clarifies why the product of the three indicators mathematically equals the number of wind power technology patents—each indicator quantifies the relative size of one layer with respect to the layer immediately surrounding it.

This calculation formula shows that the number of wind power technology patent applications can be decomposed into three factors: (1) the relative priority of wind power technology within renewable energy technology $\frac{\text{PATENT}_{\text{WIND}}}{\text{PATENT}_{\text{RENEWABLE}}}$, (2) the relative priority of renewable energy technology within total patent applications $\frac{\text{PATENT}_{\text{RENEWABLE}}}{\text{PATENT}_{\text{TOTAL}}}$, and (3) the total number of patent applications "SCALE." The third factor, total number of patent applications, can be said to have a coherent relationship with the number of researchers and R&D expenditure of Company A; thus, it is used as a proxy indicator for the scale of R&D activity. The calculation results, including the three indicators, are listed in Table 2.2. Here, the ratio is the 2025 value divided by the 2020 value and is included to examine the change in values from 2020 to 2025.

From Table 2.2, I can see that the number of wind power technology patent applications increased fourfold from 2020 to 2025. This fourfold increase equals the product of the ratios of the three factors ($400\% = 200\% \times 250\% \times 80\%$). This identity is self-evident from Eq. (2.1), but by expressing it as a product of each factor, it becomes possible to present it in an intuitively understandable form and interpret

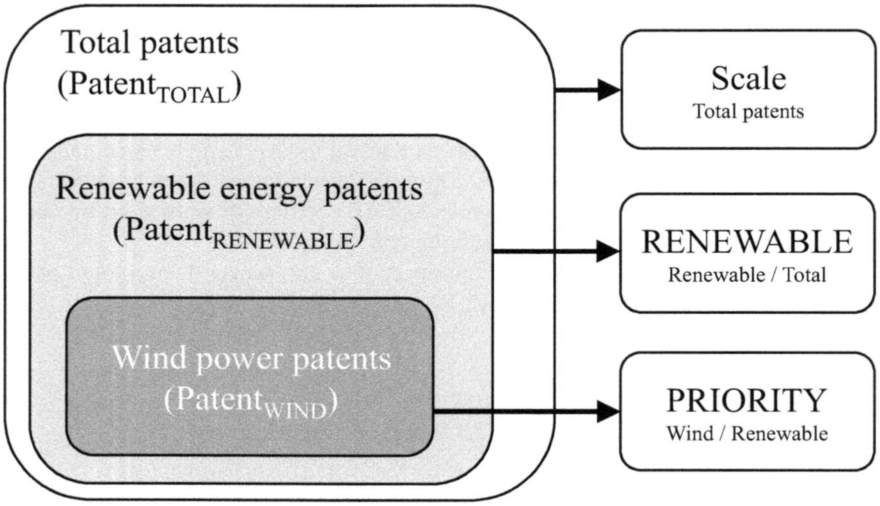

Fig. 2.1 Nested structure of patent categories and corresponding decomposition indicators. *Note* The total patent applications ($PATENT_{TOTAL}$, outer frame) contain renewable energy patents ($PATENT_{RENEWABLE}$, middle layer), which in turn contain wind power technology patents ($PATENT_{WIND}$, inner layer). Each of the three nested layers corresponds to one decomposition indicator: SCALE represents the overall R&D scale measured by total patent applications; RENEWABLE captures the relative priority of renewable energy technology within total R&D; and PRIORITY captures the relative priority of wind power technology within renewable energy R&D. The product of these three indicators equals the number of wind power technology patent applications. *Source* Created by the author

Table 2.2 Factor decomposition of wind power technology patents

Year	$PATENT_{WIND}$	PRIORITY	RENEWABLE	SCALE
2020	10	0.20	0.10	500
2025	40	0.40	0.25	400
Change ratio	400%	200%	250%	80%

the reasons for changes in patent applications for specific technologies, which is an advantageous aspect of factor decomposition analysis (Fujii & Managi, 2019).

Next, I examine each factor contributing to the increase in wind power technology patent applications. The "PRIORITY" indicator, which represents the priority of wind power within renewable energy, has a percentage of 200%, indicating that the development priority of wind power technology in Company A doubled from 2020 to 2025.

Additionally, the "RENEWABLE" indicator, which represents the relative priority of renewable energy technology within total patent applications, has a percentage of 250%, indicating that the development priority of renewable energy technology in Company A increased by 2.5 times from 2020 to 2025.

From the above, I can infer that Company A formulated a management policy that shifted its R&D strategy toward renewable energy and particularly emphasized wind power technology, as both the development priority of wind power technology and renewable energy technology increased from 2020 to 2025. However, the "SCALE" indicator, which represents the scale of R&D, decreased to 0.8 times that of the previous year, suggesting that Company A may have reduced its scale of R&D while concentrating resources intensively on wind power technology within renewable energy technologies.

In this way, factor decomposition analysis using patent information can reveal changes in R&D strategies among companies and countries. Additionally, it becomes possible to quantitatively show how patent numbers are affected by factors such as technology priority and R&D scale. Applied models of factor decomposition analysis for patent acquisition numbers and patent application numbers are introduced in Fujii (2016), Fujii and Managi (2018), and Yamashita and Fujii (2022).

2.3 Conclusion

Patent data analysis is an effective method for revealing trends and shifts in research and development strategies across various companies and industries. In particular, patent decomposition analysis provides a complementary approach for extracting meaningful information from patent data. This chapter presents a case study on wind power technology patents and demonstrates how decomposition analysis can reveal strategic shifts in research priorities and resource allocation decisions.

Patent data analysis has the potential to become a powerful methodology for transforming patent data into information about shifts in research strategy. Mastering these analytical techniques is expected to enable the identification of changes in R&D strategies across countries, regions, companies, and industries, leading to more effective resource allocation for gaining a competitive advantage. The patent decomposition framework presented in this chapter, illustrated through a simple multiplicative form for clarity of exposition, provides the conceptual foundation for the analyses developed in the subsequent chapters. When applied to multi-period changes or comparisons involving multiple technology categories, the log mean Divisia index (LMDI) method developed by Ang and Choi (1997) and systematized by Ang (2005) offers a more rigorous decomposition approach that satisfies desirable theoretical properties—including perfect decomposition without residual terms, time-reversal consistency, and aggregation consistency. In Chapters 3 onward, the LMDI method is applied to patent data from major patent offices to quantitatively separate changes in technology development priorities from changes in the overall scale of R&D activity. This methodological choice allows for a more precise understanding of how national and corporate R&D strategies have shifted over time across different environmental technology fields.

References

Ang, B. W. (2005). The LMDI approach to decomposition analysis: A practical guide. *Energy Policy, 33*(7), 867–871. https://doi.org/10.1016/j.enpol.2003.10.010

Ang, B. W., & Choi, K. H. (1997). Decomposition of aggregate energy and gas emission intensities for industry: A refined Divisia index method. *The Energy Journal, 18*(3), 59–73. https://doi.org/10.5547/ISSN0195-6574-EJ-Vol18-No3-3

Fujii, H. (2016). Decomposition analysis of green chemical technology inventions from 1971 to 2010 in Japan. *Journal of Cleaner Production, 112,* 4835–4843.

Fujii, H., & Managi, S. (2018). Trends and priority shifts in artificial intelligence technology invention: A global patent analysis. *Economic Analysis and Policy, 58,* 60–69.

Fujii, H., & Managi, S. (2019). Decomposition analysis of sustainable green technology inventions in China. *Technological Forecasting and Social Change, 139,* 10–16.

Griliches, Z. (1990). Patent statistics as economic indicators: A survey. *Journal of Economic Literature, 28*(4), 1661–1707.

Gugler, K., Szücs, F., & Wiedenhofer, T. (2024). Environmental policies and directed technological change. *Journal of Environmental Economics and Management, 124,* Article 102916.

Mejia, C., & Kajikawa, Y. (2024). Patent research in academic literature: Landscape and trends with a focus on patent analytics. *Frontiers in Research Metrics and Analytics, 9,* 1484685.

Nagaoka, S., Motohashi, K., & Goto, A. (2010). Patent data for innovation studies. *Handbook of the Economics of Innovation, 2,* 1083–1127.

Popp, D. (2002). Inducing innovation and energy prices. *The American Economic Review, 92*(1), 160–180.

Yamashita, A. S., & Fujii, H. (2022). Trend and priority change of climate change mitigation technology in the global mining sector. *Resources Policy, 78,* Article 102870.

Chapter 3
Renewable Energy Technology

3.1 Introduction

3.1.1 Background

Renewable energy technologies play a central role in addressing climate change. According to the United Nations Environment Programme (UNEP) Emissions Gap Report 2024, achieving the Paris Agreement's 1.5 °C target requires reducing greenhouse gas emissions by 42% by 2030 and 57% by 2035, necessitating a tripling of renewable energy capacity (UNEP, 2024). The pledge by over 130 countries at the COP28 climate summit in 2023 to at least triple the global renewable energy installed capacity to 11,000 GW by 2030 demonstrates the critical importance of this technological field. Recent analyses have shown that achieving carbon neutrality targets requires unprecedented scaling of renewable energy technologies (Makeeva et al., 2024).

The International Energy Agency (IEA) Renewables 2024 report predicts that, considering current policies and market conditions, approximately 5,500 GW of new renewable energy capacity will become operational by 2030 (IEA, 2024). While this amount exceeds current national targets by approximately 25%, it falls short of the tripling goal. However, recent progress has been remarkable, with solar and wind power combined projected to surpass hydroelectric power by 2024 and renewable energy generation expected to overtake coal-fired power generation by 2025. Beyond these aggregate capacity targets, the geographical and socioeconomic dimensions of renewable energy deployment also merit attention.

The importance of renewable energy technologies extends beyond climate change mitigation. Particularly in developing countries, distributed renewable energy systems, which do not require substantial capital investment in centralized infrastructure, such as large-scale thermal power plants, play a crucial role in promoting rural electrification. According to World Bank reports, 365 million people in eastern and southern Africa alone lack access to electricity, with more than 500 million people

H. Fujii, *Key Drivers of Environmental Innovation*,
https://doi.org/10.1007/978-981-92-0060-3_3

living without electricity across sub-Saharan Africa (World Bank, 2022). In these regions, distributed renewable energy systems centered on solar power represent the most cost-effective means of rapidly and efficiently providing electricity access without needing to wait for national grid expansion.

3.1.2 Literature Review: Patent Analysis in Renewable Energy Technology

Against this background, this chapter focuses on the research and development and diffusion of renewable energy technologies, explaining trends in technological development and changes in R&D priorities using patent information. Patent data serve as important indicators for evaluating the development of renewable energy technology. According to the joint report "Patents and the Energy Transition" by the IEA and European Patent Office (EPO), patent information provides solid statistical evidence of technological progress (IEA & EPO, 2021).

A substantial body of scholarship has employed patent data to analyze innovation dynamics in renewable energy technologies. These studies have yielded important insights into the relationship between policy instruments and technological innovation, the competitive landscape across countries and technology domains, and the methodological approaches for extracting meaningful signals from patent databases. The following discussion synthesizes the key findings from this literature, which provides the analytical foundation for the present chapter.

Johnstone et al. (2010) analyzed environmental policy impacts on renewable energy innovation across 25 countries (1978–2003), demonstrating that policy effectiveness varies by technology type. Broad instruments such as tradable energy certificates drive innovation in fossil fuel-competitive technologies, while targeted subsidies such as feed-in tariffs are essential for higher-cost technologies such as solar power. Nesta et al. (2014) examined technological transitions using 5,471 European firms' patents (1978–2006), revealing that small specialized firms' entry after 2000 significantly narrowed the gap in the number of fossil fuel–renewable energy patents.

Kim and Cho (2025) examined 194,485 patents (1975–2024), identifying a post-2010 surge with solar technology dominating at 60%. Their portfolio analysis confirmed U.S. leadership in terms of activity and quality, China's quantitative expansion, and Europe's qualitative excellence. Jiang et al. (2022) applied text mining to six renewable technologies (1970–2019) and reported that while solar and wind dominate and biomass remains in the growth stage, Chinese patents—despite rapid policy-driven expansion—lag developed nations in high-value innovations.

Zhang et al. (2022) developed a methodology that combines technology convergence and scientific citation analysis to identify radical solar innovations and demonstrated that cross-domain knowledge integration drives breakthrough developments. Trappey et al. (2019) applied unsupervised machine learning to 2280 patents and 5610 papers (2008–2018), revealing an emphasis on solar hydraulic storage systems. de

Paulo et al. (2023) applied social network analysis to IPC Green Inventory patents to characterize evolutionary patterns and technology roadmaps.

Hsieh et al. (2024) proposed main path and word cloud analysis for predicting emerging patent domains using 40,827 papers and 72,979 patents and calculated publication-to-patent time lags to forecast technology trends. Fung et al. (2023) demonstrated that conventional CPC/IPC codes (F03D, Y02E 10/70) underrepresent the number of wind patents by 7.5%, particularly when the number of Chinese applications and post-2010 publications are underestimated. Joo et al. (2022) analyzed patents from 2010–2021, revealing China's 48% dominance and identifying "wind turbines with rotation axes along the wind direction" as the central convergence node, with strong connections to power conversion and building integration technologies.

3.1.3 Global Trends in Renewable Energy Patent Applications

As shown in Fig. 3.1, the number of patent applications related to renewable energy technologies showed remarkable growth through the late 2000s. This period coincides with the promotion of large-scale renewable energy development projects, including the 2009 American Recovery and Reinvestment Act in the United States. The total number of patent applications peaked between 2011 and 2012, with more than 8,000 applications recorded annually. In terms of technology category, solar technology accounted for the largest share, followed by wind, biofuels, and other technologies. This surge provides empirical evidence that active fiscal support and R&D investment promotion policies by various governments effectively stimulate technological innovation.

However, after peaking in 2012, the number of patent applications showed a declining trend. This decline was particularly pronounced in solar technology and was influenced by multiple factors. First, the sharp demand downturn in the European solar power market is relevant. Spain promoted large-scale solar power introduction through feed-in tariff (FIT) schemes in the late 2000s, but excessive subsidy spending strained public finances, leading the government to implement substantial subsidy reductions and retroactive policy changes after 2010. This policy reversal severely damaged investor confidence and created negative ripple effects across the European solar power market. Germany, Italy, and other European countries also implemented similar subsidy reductions because of fiscal constraints, causing an overall European market contraction. In addition, similar FIT policy adjustments occurred across Europe, with retroactive subsidy cuts in multiple countries creating significant uncertainty for renewable energy investors (del Río & Mir-Artigues, 2014). These empirical patterns are consistent with the findings of Johnstone et al. (2010), who demonstrated that targeted policy instruments such as feed-in tariffs are particularly critical for sustaining innovation in higher-cost renewable technologies.

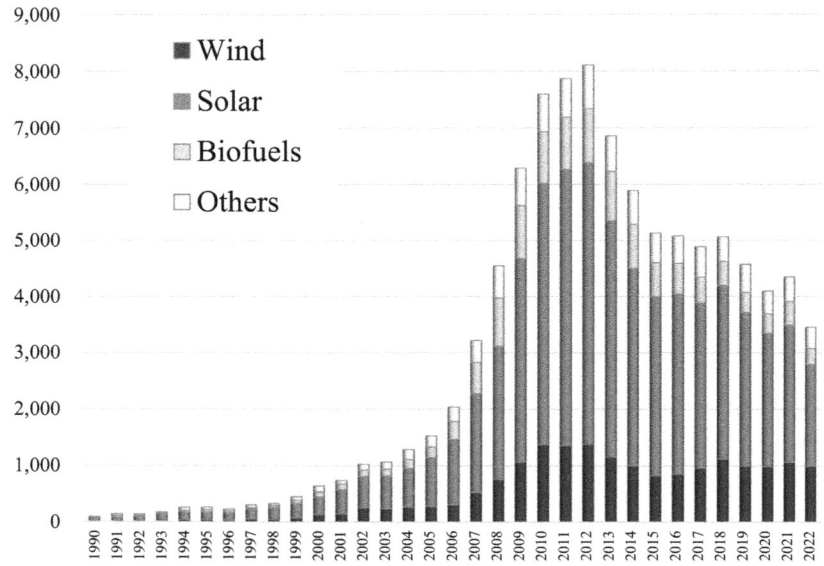

Fig. 3.1 Number of patent applications related to renewable energy technology in the patent cooperation treaty. *Note* The apparent decline in patent applications observed in 2022 should be interpreted with caution. Under standard patent procedures, applications are typically not published until 18 months after the filing date. Consequently, a substantial proportion of applications filed in 2021 and 2022 may not yet be reflected in the database at the time of data retrieval, leading to an undercount of recent filings. *Source* OECD, STI Microdata Lab: Intellectual Property Database, http://oe.cd/ipstats, created by the author

Second, the stabilization of fossil fuel prices after 2014, particularly the significant decrease in crude oil prices, reduced investment incentives for renewable energy. Crude oil prices plummeted from over $100 per barrel in mid-2014 to the $30 range in early 2016, with natural gas prices showing similar declines. This decrease in the price of fossil fuels relatively reduced the economic attractiveness of future energy cost savings through renewable energy, dampening corporate R&D investment willingness. The shale gas revolution in the United States further contributed to decreased fossil fuel prices during this period, fundamentally altering the economic landscape for renewable energy investment (Wang & Krupnick, 2015).

The decline in patent applications after 2012 shown in Fig. 3.1 and the downward trend in the share of total renewable energy patents for solar power shown in Fig. 3.2 indicate that such market environment changes, policy uncertainty, and technological maturation had a direct impact on technological innovation activities. Notably, while the share of solar patents declined from its peak of approximately 62% in 2010–2012, the relative share of wind power patents exhibited a gradual increase during the same period, rising from around 17% to over 25% by the early 2020s. This shift suggests a reallocation of R&D priorities within the renewable energy sector, with wind power—particularly offshore wind technology—emerging as a relatively more

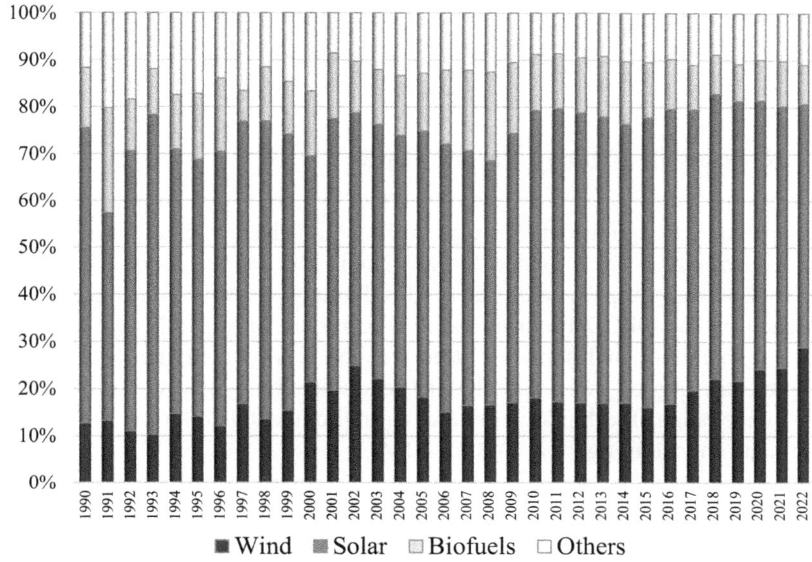

Fig. 3.2 Share of patent applications related to renewable energy technology in the patent cooperation treaty. *Source* OECD, STI Microdata Lab: Intellectual Property Database, http://oe.cd/ipstats, created by the author

active area of innovation. The divergent trajectories of solar and wind patent shares underscore the importance of disaggregated analysis in understanding the evolving landscape of renewable energy R&D.

3.1.4 Objective and Structure of This Chapter

This chapter investigates research and development in renewable energy technologies, revealing predominant trends in technological progress and shifts in R&D priorities through the lens of patent data. The analysis covers four distinct renewable energy technologies: wind power, solar power, biomass, and other renewable energy sources. Through analysis of patent trends across major intellectual property offices—including the China National Intellectual Property Administration (CNIPA), the United States Patent and Trademark Office (USPTO), the European Patent Office (EPO), the Japan Patent Office (JPO), and the Korean Intellectual Property Office (KIPO)—critical insights into the global innovation landscape within the renewable energy technology sector are provided.

The following sections present a detailed decomposition analysis of renewable energy patent trends. This approach enables a systematic examination of how national innovation systems, policy frameworks, and technological trajectories interact to shape the global renewable energy R&D landscape.

3.2 Renewable Energy Patent Data

I used patent application data from the patent statistics on environmental-related technologies, which are provided by the OECD STI Microdata Lab: Intellectual Property Database (http://oe.cd/ipstats). This dataset is constructed using algorithms developed by the OECD Environmental Directorate. Specifically, the OECD has identified patents in environment-related technologies by applying detailed search strategies, drawing on more than 200,000 classification symbols. These strategies cover a wide range of technologies related to environmental pollution, water scarcity and climate change mitigation (OECD, 2024).

Using International Patent Classification (IPC) analysis, renewable energy technologies are classified into four major sectors: Solar power, biofuels, wind energy, and other renewable energy (including geothermal, marine, and hydro energy). Table 3.1 shows the patent classification of renewable energy technologies using the IPC defined by the OECD. This study focuses on four renewable energy technology groups: (1) wind power technology (WIND), (2) solar power technology (SOLAR), (3) biofuel technology (BIOFUEL), and (4) other renewable energy technology (OTHER).

Table 3.1 Group of renewable energy technologies

Group	Technology	Definition (IPC code)
Wind	Wind energy	Y02E10/70-76
Solar	Solar thermal	Y02E10/40-47
	Solar photovoltaic (PV) energy	Y02E10/50-56
	Solar thermal-PV hybrids	Y02E10/60
Biofuels	Biofuels	Y02E50/10
Others	Geothermal energy	Y02E10/10
	Marine energy	Y02E10/30
	Hydro energy	Y02E10/20

Source OECD, STI Microdata Lab: Intellectual Property Database, http://oe.cd/ipstats, created by the author https://stats.oecd.org/wbos/fileview2.aspx?IDFile=c5c477c0-d300-42fe-af1f-d4a450c79a39

3.3 Patent Decomposition Analysis of Renewable Energy Technology

To clarify the influential factors driving patenting trends in renewable energy technologies, this section employs a factor decomposition framework to identify key drivers of innovation. While the conceptual foundation of patent decomposition analysis is established in Chap. 2, this chapter specifically applies the Logarithmic Mean Divisia Index (LMDI) method to analyze the development of these technologies. The following four indicators are utilized to evaluate technological progress:

The PRIORITY indicator is defined as the number of specific renewable energy patent applications (e.g., wind power) divided by the total number of renewable energy patent applications. This indicator provides the proportion of specific renewable energy patent applications from the total number of renewable energy patents. If the number of specific renewable energy patent applications increases more quickly than the total number of renewable energy patent applications does, then inventors are concentrating their research resources on specific types of renewable energy technology inventions, and the PRIORITY indicator will increase.

Similarly, the RENEWABLE indicator is defined as the total number of renewable energy patent applications divided by the total number of environmentally related patent applications. This indicator indicates the proportion of renewable energy patents among all environmentally related patents. It increases if the total number of renewable energy patent applications increases more quickly than the total number of environmental-related patent applications does, indicating that inventors are focusing their research resources on renewable energy technology rather than other environmental technologies.

Next, the ENVIRONMENT indicator is defined as the relative importance of environmental technology among total patent inventions. This indicator increases if the number of environmental technology patent applications increases more quickly than the total number of patent applications does. It shows how patent applicants are changing the priority of technological importance for environmental technologies relative to patents as a whole.

Finally, the SCALE indicator is defined as the total number of patent applications and thus represents the scale of national research and development (R&D) activity. This indicator is affected by macro factors such as environmental policies, fluctuations in the price of resources, and economic conditions.

Here, I introduce a decomposition approach using the wind power technology group as a specific type of renewable energy application. The number of wind power technology patent applications ($\mathrm{PATENT_{WIND}}$) is decomposed using the total number of renewable energy patent applications ($\mathrm{PATENT_{RENEW}}$), the total number of environmental-related patent applications ($\mathrm{PATENT_{ENV}}$), and the total number of patent applications ($\mathrm{PATENT_{TOTAL}}$), as shown in the decomposition equation.

$$\mathrm{PATENT_{WIND}} = \frac{\mathrm{PATENT_{WIND}}}{\mathrm{PATENT_{RENEW}}} \times \frac{\mathrm{PATENT_{RENEW}}}{\mathrm{PATENT_{ENV}}}$$

$$\times \frac{\mathrm{PATENT_{ENV}}}{\mathrm{PATENT_{TOTAL}}} \times \mathrm{PATENT_{TOTAL}}$$
$$= \mathrm{PRIORITY} \times \mathrm{RENEWABLE} \times \mathrm{ENVIRONMENT} \times \mathrm{SCALE} \tag{3.1}$$

I consider the change in wind power technology patent applications from year t ($\mathrm{PATENT}^{t}_{WIND}$) to year $t+1$ ($\mathrm{PATENT}^{t+1}_{WIND}$). The change in wind power technology patent applications can be represented using Eq. (3.1) as follows.

$$\frac{\mathrm{PATENT}^{t+1}_{WIND}}{\mathrm{PATENT}^{t}_{WIND}} = \frac{\mathrm{PRIORITY^{t+1}}}{\mathrm{PRIORITY^{t}}} \times \frac{\mathrm{RENEWABLE^{t+1}}}{\mathrm{RENEWABLE^{t}}} \times \frac{\mathrm{ENVIRONMENT^{t+1}}}{\mathrm{ENVIRONMENT^{t}}} \times \frac{\mathrm{SCALE^{t+1}}}{\mathrm{SCALE^{t}}} \tag{3.2}$$

By transforming Eq. (3.2) into a natural logarithmic function, I can obtain Eq. (3.3).

$$\ln\left(\mathrm{PATENT}^{t+1}_{WIND}\right) - \ln\left(\mathrm{PATENT}^{t}_{WIND}\right) = \ln\left(\frac{\mathrm{PRIORITY}^{t+1}}{\mathrm{PRIORITY}^{t}}\right) + \ln\left(\frac{RENEWABLE^{t+1}}{RENEWABLE^{t}}\right) + \ln\left(\frac{\mathrm{EN}VIRONMENT^{t+1}}{\mathrm{ENVIRONMENT}^{t}}\right) + \ln\left(\frac{\mathrm{SCALE}^{t+1}}{\mathrm{SCALE}^{t}}\right) \tag{3.3}$$

Multiplying both sides of Eq. (3.3) by $\omega_t^{t+1} = (\mathrm{PATENT}^{t+1}_{WIND} - \mathrm{PATENT}^{t}_{WIND})/\{\ln(\mathrm{PATENT}^{t+1}_{WIND}) - \ln(\mathrm{PATENT}^{t}_{WIND})\}$ yields Eq. (3.4) as follows.

$$\mathrm{PATENT}^{t+1}_{WIND} - \mathrm{PATENT}^{t}_{WIND} = \Delta\mathrm{PATENT}^{t,\,t+1}_{WIND} = \omega_{\mathrm{t}}^{\mathrm{t+1}}\ln\left(\frac{\mathrm{PRIORITY^{t+1}}}{\mathrm{PRIORITY^{t}}}\right) + \omega_{\mathrm{t}}^{\mathrm{t+1}}\ln\left(\frac{\mathrm{RENEWABLE^{t+1}}}{\mathrm{RENEWABLE^{t}}}\right) + \omega_{\mathrm{t}}^{\mathrm{t+1}}\ln\left(\frac{\mathrm{ENVIRONMENT^{t+1}}}{\mathrm{ENVIRONMENT^{t}}}\right) + \omega_{\mathrm{t}}^{\mathrm{t+1}}\ln\left(\frac{\mathrm{SCALE^{t+1}}}{\mathrm{SCALE^{t}}}\right) \tag{3.4}$$

Therefore, changes in the number of patent applications for wind power technologies ($\mathrm{PATENT_{WIND}}$) are decomposed based on changes in PRIORITY (first term), RENEWABLE (second term), ENVIRONMENT (third term), and SCALE (fourth term).

3.4 Comparative Analysis of Renewable Energy Patent Application

3.4.1 Comparative Analysis of IP5 Patent Invention Strategies

An analysis of the total number of renewable energy patent applications in five major patent offices from 1990 to 2022 reveals significant regional differences. As shown in Table 3.2, the China National Intellectual Property Administration (CNIPA) recorded the highest number of patent applications at 250,703, followed by the United States Patent and Trademark Office (USPTO) at 125,641, the Japan Patent Office (JPO) at 98,905, the Korean Intellectual Property Office (KIPO) at 74,435, and the European Patent Office (EPO) at 68,794.

The CNIPA's patent application numbers account for approximately 68% as large as the combined total of the other four patent offices, indicating that China is extremely active in terms of patent activities in the renewable energy technology field. This overwhelming difference in application numbers reflects the influence of the Chinese government's aggressive renewable energy promotion policies and support systems that encourage domestic patent applications.

Examining the composition ratio by technology field reveals interesting patterns among patent offices. Solar technology accounts for the largest share among all patent offices, with the highest being in the JPO at 71%, followed by the KIPO at 68%, the USPTO at 64%, the CNIPA at 60%, and the EPO at 54%. This trend suggests that solar power generation technology is technically mature and has diverse application

Table 3.2 Number of renewable energy patent applications from 1990 to 2022

Patent office		Total	Wind	Solar	Biofuel	Others
CNIPA	Patent	250,703	51,089	150,287	19,418	29,909
	Share	100%	20%	60%	8%	12%
USPTO	Patent	125,641	21,714	80,492	13,313	10,122
	Share	100%	17%	64%	11%	8%
EPO	Patent	68,794	17,360	37,433	8153	5848
	Share	100%	25%	54%	12%	9%
JPO	Patent	98,905	10,681	69,803	7956	10,465
	Share	100%	11%	71%	8%	11%
KIPO	Patent	74,435	10,282	50,438	4749	8966
	Share	100%	14%	68%	6%	12%

Note Share represents the percentage of patent applications for each technology of total renewable energy technology

Source OECD, STI Microdata Lab: Intellectual Property Database, http://oe.cd/ipstats, created by the author

possibilities. The share of wind technology is highest in the EPO at 25%, followed by the CNIPA at 20%, the USPTO at 17%, the KIPO at 14%, and the JPO at 11%. The relatively high share of wind technology in the EPO is considered related to Europe's aggressive development of offshore wind power. Europe particularly leads the world in offshore wind power development centered on the North Sea, with active technological innovation in this field.

An analysis of the trends in patent applications at three time points—the 2000s, 2010s, and 2020s—as shown in Fig. 3.3, reveals contrasting trends among patent offices. With respect to the four patent offices, the USPTO, EPO, JPO, and KIPO, applications peaked in the early 2010s but then showed a decreasing trend. This trend is more apparent in the annual transition graph, with a peak occurring in approximately 2010 and 2012 and then a declining or stagnating trend after 2013. The USPTO peaked at approximately 9000 in 2012 and then decreased to 3000 by 2022. Similarly, the EPO, JPO, and KIPO each recorded peaks of 5000–7000 between 2010 and 2012 and then decreased to 1000–2500 by 2022.

The major factors driving this declining trend include, first, the demand downturn in the European solar power market, which peaked in 2012, as mentioned earlier. Policy changes represented by Spain's failed feed-in tariff system and the stabilization of fossil fuel prices after 2014 reduced investment incentives for renewable energy. Second, major technology fields, particularly solar power, reached a certain maturity stage, relatively reducing opportunities for innovative patent applications. Third, reductions in R&D investment and subsidy cuts for innovative projects following the 2008 global financial crisis may have had an impact.

The patent application trends for the CNIPA show a completely different pattern from those for the other four patent offices. The number of applications, which was approximately 2000 annually in the 2000s, increased dramatically in the 2010s

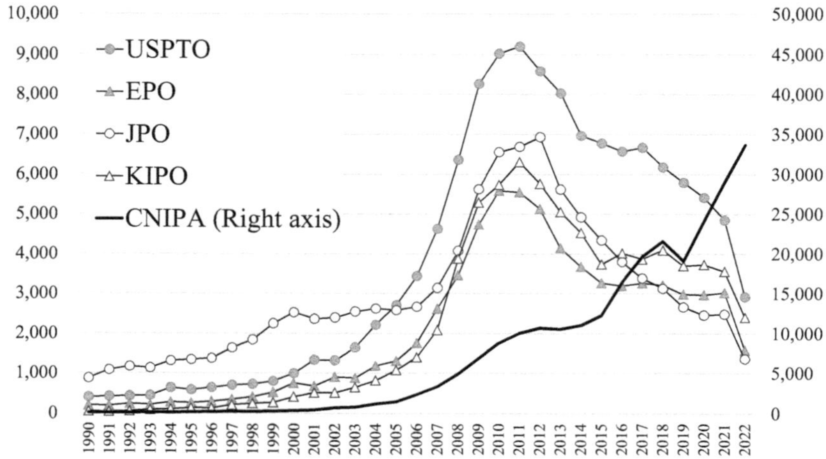

Fig. 3.3 Number of patent applications related to renewable energy technology in the IP5. *Source* OECD, STI Microdata Lab: Intellectual Property Database, http://oe.cd/ipstats, created by the author

and reached levels exceeding 30,000 in the 2020s. The graph shows an upward trend starting in approximately 2010, with particularly dramatic increases after 2016. Notably, although there was a temporary decrease in 2019, the number of applications increased again after 2020.

This surge in patent applications in China can be explained by multiple policy and institutional factors. First, the Chinese government positioned renewable energy as a strategic priority field in its Five-Year Plans, providing aggressive support. In particular, since the 12th Five-Year Plan (2011–2015), the cultivation of the new energy industry has clearly been positioned as a national strategy, and the 13th Five-Year Plan (2016–2020) set substantial expansion targets for renewable energy. The 14th Five-Year Plan (2021–2025) also positioned renewable energy development as a top priority for achieving the "dual carbon targets" of peaking carbon emissions by 2030 and achieving carbon neutrality by 2060 that were announced in September 2020.

Second, since the late 2000s, China has introduced various support systems that encourage patent applications. Subsidies for patent application costs to enterprises and research institutions, tax incentives for patent acquisition, and personnel systems using patent numbers as criteria for performance evaluation and promotion promoted the surge in the number of patent applications. However, while these systems emphasized quantitative expansion, they did not address challenges regarding the qualitative aspects of patents. China's green patent examination system, which was established in 2012, provides accelerated review processes for renewable energy technologies, thus reducing examination periods (Xu et al., 2024).

Third, regarding the temporary decrease in 2019, the impact of the U.S.–China trade friction that began in 2017 can be considered. Trade friction heightened uncertainty about Chinese companies' R&D investment and international expansion, potentially temporarily suppressing patent application activities. However, the surge in these activities after 2020 can be interpreted as reflecting the Chinese government's strengthened stance on reinforcing domestic technology foundations and technological independence.

3.4.2 Comparative Analysis of Technology Field Shares

The chronological changes in the number of patents and share for the technology fields shown in Figs. 3.4a and b indicate shifts in strategic priorities within renewable energy technology development. In all the patent offices, the relative share of wind power technology tends to increase from the 2000s to the 2020s. This trend is particularly pronounced for the EPO and can be explained by multiple technological and market factors.

First, the rapid increase in demand for offshore wind power technology is notable. In Europe, particularly in North Sea coastal countries (UK, Germany, Denmark, Netherlands), large-scale offshore wind power projects have been initiated one after another, accelerating associated technological innovation. Compared with onshore

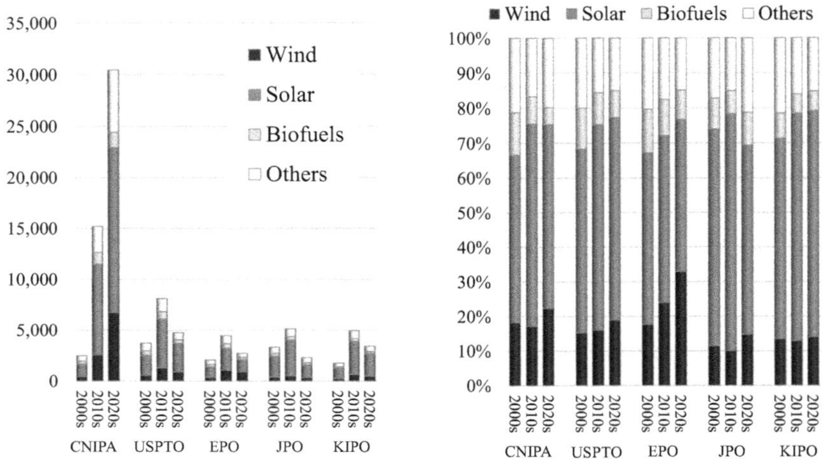

Fig. 3.4 Number and share of patent applications for three types of renewable energy. *Source* OECD, STI Microdata Lab: Intellectual Property Database, http://oe.cd/ipstats, created by the author

wind, offshore wind power presents new technological development challenges, including larger turbine design, floating foundation structures, and materials and construction technologies adapted to marine environments, thus stimulating patent applications. The EPO-IRENA joint patent insights report confirms that the number of offshore wind patent applications surged between 2006 and 2012, stagnated until 2017, and then witnessed renewed growth, with Europe, Asia, and the U.S. emerging as major innovation hubs (Schaaf et al., 2024; IRENA & EPO, 2023).

Second, continuous technology development toward larger and more efficient wind turbines is progressing. In the 2020s, the development of ultra large turbines exceeding 15 MW is advancing, with innovation continuing across diverse technology fields, including blade design, drivetrain technology, and power conversion systems.

Third, compared with solar power, wind power has not progressed in terms of technology standardization and commoditization, leaving significant room for differentiation. Each manufacturer is deploying aggressive patent strategies to secure unique technological advantages.

3.5 Results of the Patent Decomposition Analysis

Figures 3.5, 3.6, 3.7, 3.8, and 3.9 show the cumulative changes in renewable energy patent applications calculated using the patent decomposition analysis. Notably, the values in Figs. 3.5, 3.6, 3.7, 3.8, and 3.9 are based on the yearly average number of patent applications from 2000 to 2009. The change from 2000s–2010s represents the change in the average annual number of patent applications from the 2000s (2000 to 2009) to the 2010s (2010 to 2019). Similarly, the change from 2010s–2020s represents the change in the average annual number of patent applications from the 2010s to the 2020s (2020 to 2022). It should be noted that while the 2000s and 2010s cover ten-year periods, the 2020s data point represents the average of the most recent three years (2020–2022) available in the dataset. The use of annual averages ensures statistical comparability across these different period lengths. The plotted dots show the estimated patent application change, with the average annual number of patent applications from the 2000s as a baseline, and the bar chart shows the contribution effects of each determinant on patent applications. The sum of the bars is equivalent to the dot.

This study set the five major patent offices—the CNIPA, USPTO, EPO, JPO, and KIPO—as the analysis targets and conducted patent decomposition analysis. The analysis focused on wind power and solar power, the two technologies that account for the majority of patents obtained in renewable energy technology.

3.5.1 Results of the Patent Decomposition Analysis for the CNIPA

As shown in Fig. 3.5, the number of patent applications for wind and solar power in China has shown a consistent upward trend from the 2000s to the 2010s and from the 2010s to the 2020s (see the dot in Fig. 3.5). However, the factors driving this increase fundamentally differ between the two periods, reflecting the evolution of China's renewable energy technology development strategy.

The increase in wind and solar power patents from the 2000s to the 2010s is driven primarily by the overwhelming contribution of the SCALE effect. This phenomenon suggests that the increase in patent numbers in the 2010s was caused mainly by a general increase in total patent numbers at CNIPA. Multiple institutional and policy factors are responsible for this increase. As mentioned in Sect. 3.4.1, China systematically introduced various support systems encouraging patent applications from the late 2000s. Tax incentives for patent acquisition, subsidies for patent application costs to enterprises and research institutions, and personnel systems using patent numbers as criteria for performance evaluation and promotion contributed to the surge in patent applications in China.

It should be noted that for solar power in the 2000s–2010s period, while the SCALE effect was the dominant driver, the ENVIRONMENT effect and PRIORITY effect also made meaningful positive contributions. The positive PRIORITY effect during this period indicates that solar technology was actively gaining priority within renewable energy patents. In contrast, the RENEWABLE effect was negative even during this period, suggesting that the relative position of renewable energy within overall environmental technology was already beginning to show signs of decline. As discussed below, the PRIORITY effect for solar power subsequently turned sharply negative in the 2010s–2020s period, underscoring a significant shift in China's renewable energy R&D strategy from solar-dominant innovation toward a more diversified technological portfolio.

In contrast, from the 2010s to the 2020s, the increase in patent applications shows a more diversified and strategic factor composition. With respect to wind power patents, PRIORITY, ENVIRONMENT, and SCALE all make positive contributions to the increase in patents, whereas RENEWABLE makes a negative contribution. These results indicate that while the relative priority of renewable energy patents among all environmental-related patents decreased in China in the 2020s, the priority of wind power technology within renewable energy clearly increased.

The background to increased wind power technology priority involves multiple strategic decisions. First, in terms of achieving the "dual carbon targets" (carbon emission peak-out by 2030 and carbon neutrality by 2060) announced by President Xi Jinping at the UN General Assembly in September 2020, wind power played an important role. Second, China became the world leader in offshore wind power installed capacity in 2021, establishing technological superiority in this field. In the 2020s, patent activities have become active in advanced technology fields such as floating offshore wind power and ultra-large turbines. Third, the construction of large-scale wind power bases in the "Three North" region (North China, Northeast, Northwest) and the Inner Mongolia Autonomous Region is advancing, increasing development demand for system technologies such as grid connection, output fluctuation countermeasures, and integration with energy storage. These targets have fundamentally reshaped China's energy technology development strategy, with the number of renewable energy patent applications increasing accordingly (Xu et al., 2024).

In contrast, for solar power technology, the PRIORITY indicator became negative in the 2020s compared with the 2010s. This represents a stark reversal from the positive PRIORITY effect observed in the 2000s–2010s period, confirming that the relative priority of solar power within renewable energy has shifted decisively downward. One reason for this result is market maturity. By 2020, the solar power industry was technologically and commercially mature, with China already occupying approximately 80% of global solar panel production capacity, establishing overwhelming market dominance. In the crystalline silicon solar cell field, efficiency improvement and cost reduction margins are limited, and opportunities for innovative patent applications have relatively decreased. Future market growth rates are also predicted to be more moderate than those of wind power.

Furthermore, the negative contribution of the RENEWABLE effect suggests a change in the relative position of renewable energy within environmental-related technologies. This change reflects that China's environmental technology policy has expanded from power generation technologies themselves to a broader range of areas. Specifically, investment has expanded across diverse environmental technology fields, such as hydrogen energy, carbon capture, utilization and storage (CCUS), smart grids, and energy efficiency technologies. The magnitude of the negative RENEWABLE effect is notably larger for solar power than for wind power, which

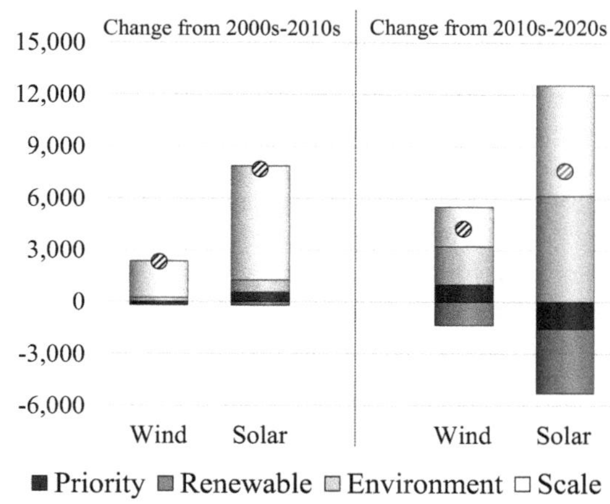

Fig. 3.5 Results of the patent decomposition analysis for the CNIPA. *Note* The y-axis is standardized such that the number of patent changes in the first period is zero. The sum of the bars equals the value of the plotted points

further corroborates the finding that the shift away from renewable energy–focused innovation disproportionately affected the solar technology domain.

3.5.2 Results of the Patent Decomposition Analysis for the USPTO

As shown in Fig. 3.6, the number of wind and solar power patent applications in the United States, in contrast to China, increased from the 2000s to the 2010s but then decreased from the 2010s to the 2020s. This trend reflects changes in renewable energy technology development priorities and the market environment in the United States.

The increase in wind power patents from the 2000s to the 2010s is driven primarily by the ENVIRONMENT and RENEWABLE effects, which together account for approximately 75% of the total increase. The SCALE effect and PRIORITY effect also made positive contributions, though of smaller magnitude. This period coincides with the implementation of approximately $90 billion in renewable energy investment through the 2009 American Recovery and Reinvestment Act, when U.S. overall patent activity became active. The ENVIRONMENT effect indicates that the increase in patents across environmental-related technologies was particularly pronounced, reflecting that climate change countermeasures were positioned as a national priority. Importantly, the substantial positive RENEWABLE effect demonstrates that renewable energy technologies gained increasing prominence within the broader environmental technology portfolio during this period. With respect to wind power technology, the PRIORITY effect also made a positive contribution, indicating that R&D investment in wind power was relatively emphasized among renewable energy technologies. Behind this development was the rapid deployment of onshore wind power in the vast Midwest region of the United States and increasing technology development demand during the germination period of offshore wind power projects along the Atlantic coast.

For solar power, the pattern of the 2000s–2010s increase was broadly similar to that of wind power, with all four factors making positive contributions. The ENVIRONMENT effect was the largest driver, followed by the RENEWABLE effect, the SCALE effect, and the PRIORITY effect. The positive PRIORITY effect for solar power indicates that solar technology was actively gaining relative importance within the renewable energy patent portfolio during this period, a trend that would subsequently reverse in the 2010s–2020s period.

From the 2010s to the 2020s, the number of patent applications for both wind and solar power decreased significantly. The primary driver of this decline was the substantial negative contribution of the RENEWABLE effect. The ENVIRONMENT effect also turned negative for both technologies. In contrast, the SCALE effect remained marginally positive for both wind and solar, indicating that overall U.S. patent activity did not contract but rather continued to expand slightly. The PRIORITY effect diverged between the two technologies: positive for wind but negative for solar.

The overwhelmingly negative RENEWABLE effect is the most striking feature of this period, accounting for the majority of patent declines in both wind and solar technologies. This finding indicates that the relative priority of renewable energy technologies decreased sharply within the environmental technology domain. Multiple factors contributed to this shift. The decreased priority of climate change countermeasures during the Trump administration, the reduction in renewable energy support measures by the federal government, and the policy shift favoring the fossil fuel industry all contributed to the diminished position of renewable energy within the U.S. innovation system. The announcement of withdrawal from the Paris Agreement in 2017 was a symbolic event marking this policy shift. Importantly, these policy changes did not reduce overall U.S. patent activity—as evidenced by the positive SCALE effect—but rather redirected innovation efforts away from renewable energy technologies toward other technological domains.

The negative contribution of the ENVIRONMENT effect indicates that the relative importance of environmental-related patents among all patents also decreased, though to a lesser extent than the RENEWABLE effect. This decrease reflects not only the decreased policy commitment to climate change countermeasures but also reduced investment incentives for clean energy technologies because of the stabilization and decline of fossil fuel prices after 2014. Natural gas is abundantly and cheaply supplied because the shale gas revolution has relatively reduced the economic attractiveness of renewable energy.

The combined negative contributions of the RENEWABLE and ENVIRONMENT effects suggest that the U.S. innovation system experienced a twofold contraction: a decline in the priority of environmental technologies within the overall patent landscape, compounded by a decline in the priority of renewable energy within environmental technologies. This phenomenon may reflect a shift in the focus of R&D investment from power generation technologies to optimization technologies for a broader energy system, including energy storage, smart grids, demand-side management.

Fourth, with respect to the PRIORITY effect, wind power makes a positive contribution while solar power makes a negative contribution. The increase in the relative priority of wind power technology is related to the development stage of offshore wind power technology. Offshore wind power has significant room for technological innovation, including large turbine design, floating foundation structures, and marine environment adaptation technologies, thus maintaining importance in terms of patent strategies. In contrast, solar power technology is approaching market maturity, with the marginal revenue of patent applications in standard technologies declining, which manifests as a negative contribution of the PRIORITY effect. This divergence in the PRIORITY effect between wind and solar power parallels the pattern observed in China's CNIPA analysis, suggesting that the relative shift in R&D emphasis from solar to wind power is a global phenomenon driven by differences in technological maturity rather than country-specific policy factors alone.

It is instructive to compare the USPTO results with those of the CNIPA. While both patent offices show a negative RENEWABLE effect in the 2010s–2020s period, the underlying dynamics differ markedly. In China, the SCALE effect remained strongly positive, reflecting continued expansion of overall patent activity. In the United States, the SCALE effect was negligible, indicating stagnation in overall patent growth. Moreover, the ENVIRONMENT effect was strongly positive in China but negative in the United States, highlighting a fundamental divergence in the two countries' policy orientation toward environmental technology. These contrasting patterns underscore how national innovation systems and policy frameworks shape the composition of renewable energy patent activities in fundamentally different ways.

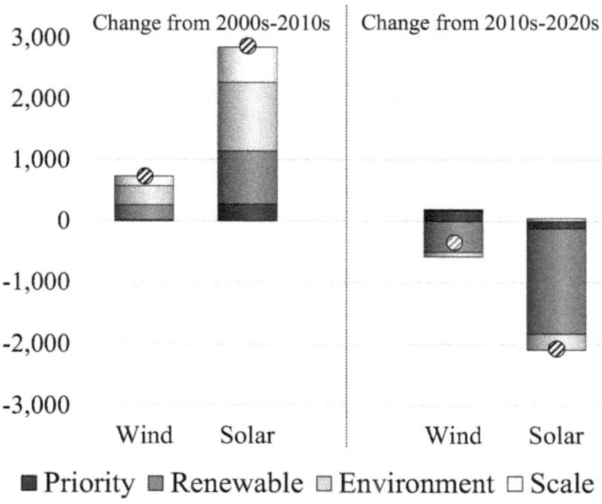

Fig. 3.6 Results of the patent decomposition analysis for the USPTO. *Note* The y-axis is standardized such that the number of patent changes in the first period is zero. The sum of the bars equals the value of the plotted points

3.5.3 *Results of the Patent Decomposition Analysis for the EPO*

As shown in Fig. 3.7, the number of wind and solar power patent applications in Europe shows trends similar to those of the United States, increasing from the 2000s to the 2010s and then showing a notable declining trend from the 2010s to the 2020s. However, Europe-specific factor compositions are observed, with particularly characteristic patterns in wind power technology.

The increase in wind power patents from the 2000s to the 2010s shows an interesting pattern in which all four decomposition factors make positive contributions: ENVIRONMENT was the largest driver, followed by PRIORITY, RENEWABLE, and SCALE. The positive contribution of the SCALE effect indicates the overall activation of patent activity in Europe during this period. From the late 2000s to the early 2010s, the European Union positioned climate change countermeasures as the top priority policy issue, setting "20-20-20 targets" for 2020. This clear policy commitment stimulated R&D investment across environmental technologies.

For solar power, the overall increase was driven by positive contributions from the ENVIRONMENT, RENEWABLE, and SCALE effects. However, the PRIORITY effect was negative, indicating that the relative priority of solar technology within the renewable energy patent portfolio was already declining in Europe during this earlier period. This contrasts with the CNIPA and USPTO, where the solar PRIORITY effect was positive in the 2000s–2010s period. The early onset of negative PRIORITY for solar power in Europe likely reflects the fact that European solar manufacturers faced competitive pressure from Chinese producers at an earlier stage, and that the European innovation system began shifting its renewable energy R&D emphasis toward wind power—particularly offshore wind—sooner than other major patent offices.

The positive contributions of ENVIRONMENT and RENEWABLE effects indicate that environmental-related technologies, particularly renewable energy technologies, occupied a core position in Europe's technology development strategy. In Europe, a comprehensive climate change countermeasures framework has been constructed, including the introduction of the Emissions Trading System (EU-ETS), strict environmental regulations, and renewable energy directives, strongly promoting technological innovation.

From the 2010s to the 2020s, the number of patent applications for both wind and solar power decreased significantly. The primary driver of this decline was the substantial negative contribution of the RENEWABLE effect. However, not all decomposition factors were negative. The SCALE effect remained positive for both technologies, and the PRIORITY effect for wind power was strongly positive. For wind power in particular, the positive contributions of PRIORITY and SCALE partially offset the negative RENEWABLE effect. For solar power, only the SCALE effect was positive, while both PRIORITY and RENEWABLE were negative, resulting in a larger net decline.

The overwhelmingly negative RENEWABLE effect is the most critical factor in the decline of both wind and solar patents at the EPO. This change was significantly influenced by the European debt crisis (Eurozone crisis) of the 2010s. Between 2010 and 2012, southern European countries such as Greece, Spain, Italy, and Portugal faced serious fiscal crises, forcing austerity fiscal policies. As a result, subsidies for renewable energy were substantially reduced, and investment rapidly decreased. Spain, in particular, was the world's largest solar power market in 2008, but its market suffered devastating damage from subsidy reductions and retroactive policy changes after 2010. This policy reversal severely damaged investor confidence and created a negative ripple effect on renewable energy investment across Europe.

Additionally, this event reflects not only R&D budget cuts due to fiscal constraints but also the relative decrease in the economic attractiveness of renewable energy due to the decline in fossil fuel prices after 2014. Furthermore, European renewable energy technologies are considered to have reached a certain maturity stage, thereby reducing opportunities for innovative patent applications.

Regarding the PRIORITY effect from the 2010s to the 2020s, wind power shows a strongly positive contribution while solar power shows a negative contribution. This difference reflects differences in maturity and market trends between the two technologies. Wind power, particularly offshore wind power, is still recognized as a growth field in Europe. Europe accounts for approximately 70% of global offshore wind power capacity, with the UK, Germany, Denmark, and the Netherlands promoting large-scale projects. Offshore wind power has significant room for technological innovation, including large turbines, floating foundation structures, and grid connection technologies, with patent activities continuing.

In contrast, solar power is technically mature, and European companies have been at a disadvantage in terms of price competition with Chinese companies, particularly in the crystalline silicon solar cell field. Many European solar panel manufacturers were forced to fail or withdraw, significantly shrinking the industrial base. As noted above, the negative PRIORITY effect for solar power was already evident in the 2000s–2010s period and deepened further in the 2010s–2020s period, indicating a sustained and accelerating decline in the relative priority of solar technology within Europe's renewable energy innovation system.

3.5.4 Results of the Patent Decomposition Analysis for the JPO

As shown in Fig. 3.8, the number of patent applications in Japan for wind and solar power generation exhibits a unique trend distinct from that of other major patent offices. Notably, the SCALE factor, which contributed to patent growth in China, the United States, and Europe, is negative across all periods and both technologies. This persistent negative SCALE effect indicates a contraction of overall patent activity in Japan, reflecting the prolonged economic stagnation and reduced corporate R&D

Fig. 3.7 Results of the patent decomposition analysis for the EPO. *Note* The y-axis is standardized such that the number of patent changes in the first period is zero. The sum of the bars equals the value of the plotted points

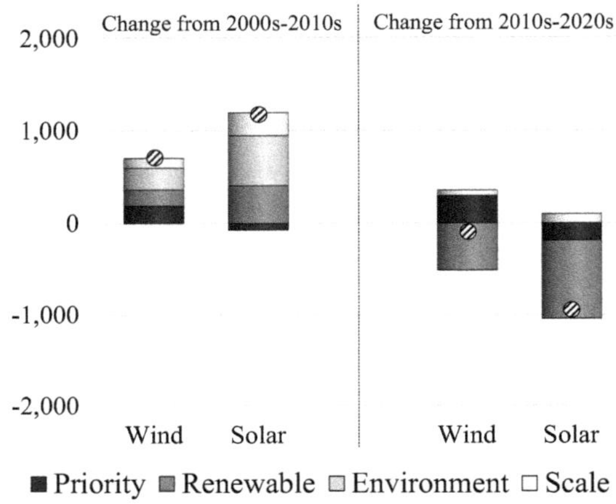

expenditure that characterized the Japanese economy during these decades. Despite the negative SCALE effect, wind power patents increased modestly from the 2000s to the 2010s. This increase was driven primarily by the RENEWABLE effect and the ENVIRONMENT effect, which together more than offset the negative contributions of SCALE and PRIORITY. The positive RENEWABLE effect indicates that renewable energy gained relative importance within environmental technologies during this period, while the negative PRIORITY effect suggests that wind power did not gain priority within the renewable energy domain—consistent with the structural constraints discussed below.

The background behind the relatively modest growth in wind power technology development in Japan is linked to the country's geographical and industrial characteristics. First, Japan has a narrow land area with many mountains, limiting the number of suitable sites for large-scale onshore wind power. Additionally, owing to the high typhoon frequency, durability against strong winds is required, thus making the costs of wind power introduction relatively high. Second, Japanese electric power companies maintained a strategy emphasizing nuclear power as a base-load power source (before the 2011 Fukushima Daiichi nuclear accident), with relatively weak investment incentives for wind power.

From the 2010s to the 2020s, wind power patents declined, driven by the large negative RENEWABLE effect and the continued negative SCALE effect. However, two notable positive contributions partially offset this decline. The PRIORITY effect turned positive, representing a significant reversal from the negative value in the previous period. This shift indicates that wind power gained increasing priority within the renewable energy patent portfolio, likely reflecting Japan's growing policy interest in offshore wind power. In 2020, the Japanese government announced the "Green Growth Strategy," which identified offshore wind power as a priority sector with a target of 30–45 GW by 2040. The ENVIRONMENT effect also remained positive, suggesting that environmental technology continued to maintain its position within overall Japanese patent activity. Nevertheless, these positive contributions were insufficient to overcome the structural headwinds of declining overall patent activity (negative SCALE) and the diminishing position of renewable energy within environmental technology (negative RENEWABLE).

With respect to solar power generation technology, the number of patent applications increased substantially from the 2000s to the 2010s. The dominant driver was the RENEWABLE effect, followed by the ENVIRONMENT effect and the PRIORITY effect. These three positive effects more than compensated for the large negative SCALE effect.

Unlike wind power, the PRIORITY and RENEWABLE effects show positive contributions from the 2000s to the 2010s, which is notable. This finding indicates that the relative priority of solar power within renewable energy technologies has increased. Behind this increase is a fundamental shift in Japan's energy policy that was triggered by the 2011 Great East Japan Earthquake and the Fukushima Daiichi nuclear accident. When the feed-in tariff (FIT) system was introduced in July 2012, the introduction of solar power expanded rapidly. In particular, high purchase price settings triggered a construction boom for mega-solar (large-scale solar power plants). Corresponding to this market expansion, technology development also became active, with patent applications made across diverse fields, including panel installation technology, grid connection technology, output prediction technology, and maintenance/operation technology. Japan's FIT system was enacted following the Fukushima nuclear accident with the explicit goal of accelerating renewable energy deployment, resulting in solar PV installations surging from 5.6 GW in 2012 to more than 50 GW by 2020 (Yamada et al., 2021). The magnitude of the ENVIRONMENT effect deserves particular attention. This large positive contribution indicates that environmental technologies as a whole gained substantial ground within overall Japanese patent activity during this period, likely driven by heightened environmental awareness and policy reorientation following the Fukushima disaster.

From the 2010s to the 2020s, solar power patents declined sharply, the largest absolute decline among all five patent offices analyzed in this chapter. The decline was driven by two dominant negative factors: the RENEWABLE effect and the PRIORITY effect, which together accounted for approximately 93% of the total decline. The SCALE effect also contributed negatively, consistent with the broader contraction of Japanese patent activity. In contrast, the ENVIRONMENT effect remained positive, indicating that environmental technology maintained its relative position within overall patent activity—a pattern similar to the EPO results and distinct from the USPTO. The sharply negative PRIORITY effect is particularly noteworthy.

During the 2010s, Japan's solar industry maintained a high technological standard but found itself at a disadvantage in international competition, particularly in terms of price competition with Chinese companies. Japanese firms such as Sharp, Kyocera, and Sanyo Electric (later integrated into Panasonic), which had once led the global market, rapidly lost market share starting in the late 2000s because of the rise of Chinese companies. This shift in the market environment likely influenced patent application activity. Furthermore, the saturation of the domestic solar market

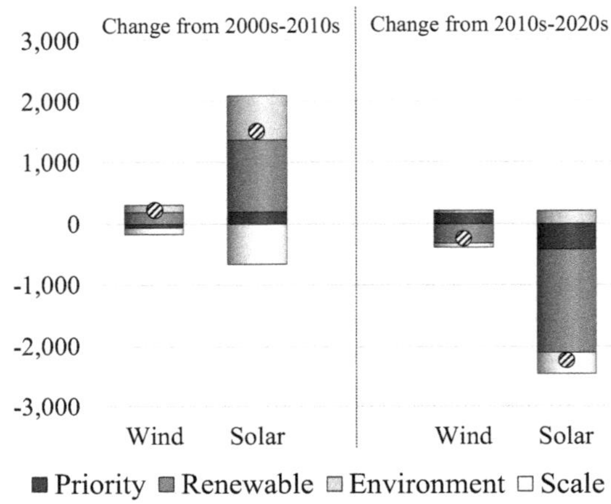

Fig. 3.8 Results of the patent decomposition analysis for the JPO. *Source* The y-axis is standardized such that the number of patent changes in the first period is zero. The sum of the bars equals the value of the plotted points

following the initial FIT-driven boom, combined with successive reductions in FIT purchase prices, reduced the incentives for continued solar R&D investment. The shift in Japan's renewable energy innovation focus toward wind power and other emerging technologies such as hydrogen and ammonia further contributed to the decline in solar patent priority.

3.5.5 Results of the Patent Decomposition Analysis for the KIPO

As shown in Fig. 3.9, the number of registered wind and solar power generation patents in South Korea tends to be similar to that in the United States and Europe, with the SCALE effect being positive in all the results. The positive contribution of the SCALE effect suggests a rapid expansion of overall patent activity in South Korea during this period. Throughout the 2000s, South Korea promoted the transition to a knowledge-based economy as a national strategy and significantly increased its research and development investment. South Korea's R&D expenditure as a percentage of GDP rose from approximately 2.2% in 2000 to 3.7% in 2010, reaching one of the highest levels among OECD countries. This aggressive R&D investment policy stimulated patent application activity overall.

With respect to the shift in wind power patents from the 2000s to the 2010s, the RENEWABLE, ENVIRONMENT, and SCALE effects all made positive contributions, driving the overall increase. However, the PRIORITY effect was slightly negative, indicating that wind power did not gain relative priority within the renewable energy patent portfolio during this period.

From the 2010s to the 2020s, wind power patents declined, driven primarily by the large negative RENEWABLE effect. The PRIORITY, ENVIRONMENT, and

SCALE effects all remained positive but were insufficient to offset the RENEWABLE decline. The positive PRIORITY effect, though modest, indicates that wind power gained some priority within renewable energy—a reversal from the negative value in the previous period—paralleling the pattern observed at the JPO and other patent offices. This negative RENEWABLE contribution stems from Korea's industrial structure and geographical characteristics. First, Korea possesses an export-oriented manufacturing base centered on semiconductors, displays, information and communication technology, shipbuilding, and automobiles, where R&D investment has been prioritized for these sectors. Second, South Korea has a relatively small land area, which limits the number of suitable sites for onshore wind power generation. Furthermore, compared with their European, American, and Chinese counterparts, Korean companies in the wind power industry were less competitive, and the domestic market was also limited.

A similar trend to that of wind power generation is observed in solar power generation technology. From the 2000s to the 2010s, the number of patent applications increased significantly because of positive contributions from all four factors. The positive PRIORITY effect indicates that solar power actively gained priority within renewable energy in South Korea during this period, consistent with the Korean government's promotion of solar energy as part of its "Green Growth" strategy announced in 2008.

From the 2010s to the 2020s, solar power patents declined substantially. The decline was overwhelmingly driven by the RENEWABLE effect, which alone exceeded the total decline in magnitude. While SCALE and ENVIRONMENT effects showed positive contributions, the RENEWABLE factor made a significant negative contribution. The PRIORITY effect was marginally negative, indicating that solar power's relative position within renewable energy was essentially stable—a notable contrast to the JPO, where the solar PRIORITY effect was sharply negative. This difference suggests that while Japan experienced a decisive shift in R&D priority away from solar power, South Korea maintained a relatively balanced approach to solar technology within its renewable energy portfolio.

Comparing the JPO and KIPO results reveals instructive parallels and divergences. Both offices share a common pattern of strongly negative RENEWABLE effects in the 2010s–2020s period for both technologies, confirming that the decline in renewable energy's relative position within environmental technology is an East Asian phenomenon as well as a global one. However, the two offices diverge in their SCALE effects: persistently negative at the JPO but consistently positive at the KIPO, reflecting the contrasting trajectories of overall innovation activity in the two economies. The ENVIRONMENT effect provides another point of contrast: it remained positive at both offices in the 2010s–2020s period, indicating that both countries maintained their commitment to environmental technology even as renewable energy's share within this domain declined. This pattern aligns with the EPO results and contrasts with the USPTO, where the ENVIRONMENT effect turned negative. Overall, the JPO and KIPO results suggest that the decline in renewable energy patents in Japan and South Korea was driven primarily by the reallocation of

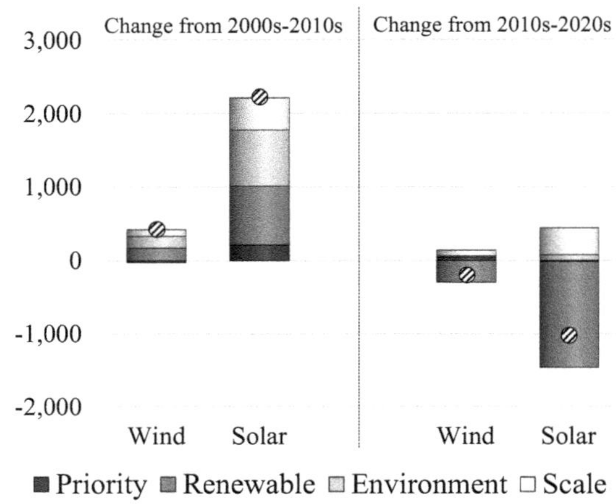

Fig. 3.9 Results of the patent decomposition analysis for the KIPO. *Note* The y-axis is standardized such that the number of patent changes in the first period is zero. The sum of the bars equals the value of the plotted points

environmental technology R&D toward non-renewable-energy domains, rather than by a retreat from environmental technology innovation itself.

3.6 Conclusion

In this chapter, patent application trends in renewable energy technologies, particularly wind and solar power, were comprehensively analyzed from the 2000s to the 2020s, targeting IP5 (USPTO, CNIPA, EPO, JPO, KIPO), using the LMDI decomposition analysis method. The analysis revealed that the renewable energy technology development priorities for each country/region have changed significantly over time. These changes moreover show different patterns depending on each country's industrial policies, market structures, technology maturity, and economic conditions.

As a first major finding, the sustained increase in the number of patent applications in China and the qualitative transformation of its factor composition can be cited. From the 2000s to the 2010s, the SCALE effect was dominant, with the number of renewable energy patents also increasing under general patent encouragement policies. It should be noted, however, that the ENVIRONMENT and PRIORITY effects also made meaningful positive contributions for solar power during this period, indicating that solar technology was actively gaining priority. From the 2010s to the 2020s, there was a transition to a more strategic factor composition, with the PRIORITY effect showing a particularly notable positive contribution to wind power technology. This observation reflects China's strategic positioning of offshore wind power as a key priority area in achieving its "dual carbon targets" (2030 carbon emission peak-out, 2060 carbon neutrality). In contrast, the PRIORITY effect for solar power technology turned negative, revealing strategic decision-making to reallocate R&D resources from solar power, where market dominance has already been established, to wind power, which has greater growth potential.

As a second important finding, the significant decrease in the number of patent applications in the United States and Europe and their multifaceted factors were revealed. In both regions, the number of patent applications decreased after peaking in approximately 2012. However, the factor compositions differed between the two regions and from the pattern initially expected. In both the United States and Europe, the SCALE effect remained marginally positive, indicating that overall patent activity did not contract. The primary driver of the decline in both regions was the strongly negative RENEWABLE effect, indicating a sharp decrease in the relative priority of renewable energy within environmental technologies. The ENVIRONMENT effect diverged: it turned negative in the United States, reflecting the decreased policy commitment to climate change countermeasures during the Trump administration and the increased economic attractiveness of fossil fuels due to the shale gas revolution, whereas it turned slightly negative or remained near-zero at the EPO in the 2010s–2020s period, consistent with Europe's sustained commitment to environmental technology through the European Green Deal and the strengthened EU-ETS. In Europe, fiscal austerity due to the Eurozone crisis in the early 2010s and policy uncertainty represented by Spain's failed feed-in tariff system severely damaged investor confidence and suppressed patent activities.

As a third finding, Japan exhibited a uniquely persistent negative SCALE effect across all periods and both technologies, distinguishing it from all other patent offices analyzed. This structural contraction of overall patent activity reflects the prolonged economic stagnation that characterized the Japanese economy. Despite this headwind, the RENEWABLE and ENVIRONMENT effects drove modest growth in patent applications during the 2000s–2010s period. The 2011 Fukushima Daiichi nuclear accident triggered a fundamental energy policy shift, with the subsequent introduction of the FIT system in 2012 generating strongly positive PRIORITY and RENEWABLE effects for solar power. However, from the 2010s to the 2020s, solar patent applications declined sharply—the largest absolute decline among all five patent offices—driven by the negative RENEWABLE and PRIORITY effects. The negative PRIORITY effect for solar power was the largest among the non-Chinese patent offices, reflecting the saturation of the domestic solar market, successive FIT purchase price reductions, and a strategic R&D shift toward wind power (as evidenced by the positive wind PRIORITY effect) and emerging technologies such as hydrogen and ammonia.

As a fourth finding, South Korea shared several patterns with Japan, including strongly negative RENEWABLE effects in the 2010s–2020s period and a reversal of the wind PRIORITY effect from negative to positive. However, the consistently positive SCALE effect at the KIPO contrasts sharply with the JPO, reflecting South Korea's aggressive R&D investment expansion and transition to a knowledge-based economy. The solar PRIORITY effect remained essentially neutral in South Korea, in marked contrast to Japan's sharply negative value, suggesting that South Korea maintained a more balanced approach to solar technology within its renewable energy portfolio.

A cross-cutting finding across all five patent offices is the divergence in the ENVIRONMENT effect, which reveals fundamentally different national orientations toward environmental technology. In China, the ENVIRONMENT effect was strongly positive, reflecting the government's aggressive promotion of environmental technology as a national strategic priority. At the EPO, JPO, and KIPO, the ENVIRONMENT effect remained positive or near-zero in the 2010s–2020s period, indicating that these countries maintained their commitment to environmental technology even as renewable energy's share within this domain declined. In contrast, the ENVIRONMENT effect turned negative at the USPTO, suggesting a broader retreat from environmental technology priorities. This divergence indicates that the decline in renewable energy patents at most offices was driven primarily by the reallocation of environmental technology R&D toward non-renewable-energy domains—such as battery technology, hydrogen energy, CCUS, and smart grids—rather than by a retreat from environmental technology innovation itself. The United States represents a partial exception, where both ENVIRONMENT and RENEWABLE effects were negative, indicating a more fundamental contraction in the prioritization of environmental and renewable energy technologies within the national innovation system.

References

de Paulo, A. F., de Oliveira Graeff, C. F., & Porto, G. S. (2023). Uncovering emerging photovoltaic technologies based on patent analysis. *World Patent Information, 73,* Article 102181.

del Río, P., & Mir-Artigues, P. (2014). Combinations of support instruments for renewable electricity in Europe: A review. *Renewable and Sustainable Energy Reviews, 40,* 287–295.

Fung, K., Goldstein, A. P., Baker, E., & Wang, Y. (2023). Rethinking the patent domains: An application to wind energy. *World Patent Information, 74,* Article 102209.

Hsieh, Y. C., Chen, S. C., & Lee, C. (2024). Forecasting patenting areas with academic paper & patent data: A wind power energy case. *World Patent Information, 78,* Article 102297.

International Energy Agency (IEA). (2024). *Renewables 2024.* IEA. https://www.iea.org/reports/renewables-2024. Accessed on February 17, 2026.

International Energy Agency (IEA) and European Patent Office (EPO). (2021). *Patents and the Energy Transition.* IEA. https://www.iea.org/reports/patents-and-the-energy-transition

IRENA & EPO. (2023). *Offshore wind energy: Patent insight report. international renewable energy agency and European patent office.* https://www.irena.org/Publications/2023/Nov/IRENA-EPO-Offshore-Wind-Energy-Patent-Insight-Report

Jiang, L., Zou, F., Qiao, Y., & Huang, Y. (2022). Patent analysis for generating the technology landscape and competition situation of renewable energy. *Journal of Cleaner Production, 378,* Article 134264.

Joo, K., Lee, M., & Lee, G. (2022). Technology originality and convergence analysis in the wind power field using patents. *Energies, 15*(9), 3316.

Johnstone, N., Haščič, I., & Popp, D. (2010). Renewable energy policies and technological innovation: Evidence based on patent counts. *Environmental and Resource Economics, 45*(1), 133–155.

Kim, S., & Cho, K. (2025). Assessing international technological competitiveness in renewable energy: An IPC-based analysis of granted patents. *Sustainability, 17*(12), 5479.

Makeeva, E., Popov, K., & Teplova, O. (2024). Patenting for profitability: Green energy innovations and firm performance in BRICS countries. *Frontiers in Environmental Science, 12,* 1332792.

Nesta, L., Vona, F., & Nicolli, F. (2014). Environmental policies, competition and innovation in renewable energy. *Journal of Environmental Economics and Management, 67*(3), 396–411.

OECD. (2024). *STI micro-data lab: Intellectual property database.* http://oe.cd/ipstats

Schaaf, J., Kasbergen, C., & van de Pas, J. (2024). Exploring macro patenting trends and key technological components in offshore wind energy. *World Patent Information, 77,* Article 102274.

Trappey, A. J. C., Chen, P. P. J., Trappey, C. V., & Ma, L. (2019). A machine learning approach for solar power technology review and patent evolution analysis. *Applied Sciences, 9*(7), 1478.

United Nations Environment Programme (UNEP). (2024). *Emissions gap report 2024: No more hot air... please!* UNEP. https://www.unep.org/resources/emissions-gap-report-2024

Wang, Z., & Krupnick, A. (2015). A retrospective review of shale gas development in the United States: What led to the boom? *Economics of Energy & Environmental Policy, 4*(1), 5–18.

World Bank. (2022, November 9). *World Bank Group announces major initiative to electrify Sub-Saharan Africa with distributed renewable energy.* https://www.worldbank.org/en/news/press-release/2022/11/09/world-bank-group-announces-major-initiative-to-electrify-sub-saharan-africa-with-distributed-renewable-energy

Xu, Q., Xie, Y., & Ying, H. (2024). Exploring the green patent system in China from the perspective of achieving the dual carbon goal: Development, challenges and prospective enhancements. *Humanities and Social Sciences Communications, 11,* 1478.

Yamada, T., Guan, D., & Fujii, M. (2021). The effects of the new Feed-in Tariff Act for solar photovoltaic (PV) energy in the wake of the Fukushima accident in Japan. *Energy Policy, 156,* Article 112447.

Zhang, Y., Zhou, L., Porter, A. L., & Guo, Y. (2022). Radical innovation detection in the solar energy domain based on patent analysis. *Frontiers in Energy Research, 10,* 1056564.

Chapter 4
Environmentally Friendly Vehicles Technology

4.1 Introduction

4.1.1 Background

The development and diffusion of environmentally friendly vehicle (EFV) technologies are pivotal to mitigating greenhouse gas (GHG) emissions within the global transportation sector. According to the International Energy Agency (IEA), the transportation sector accounts for approximately 30% of global final energy consumption and 24% of energy-related CO_2 emissions, with road transport being the primary contributor (IEA, 2024a). To align with the climate goals set forth in the Paris Agreement, a radical decarbonization of road transport by 2030 is imperative. This necessitates a decisive shift away from conventional internal combustion engine vehicles (ICEVs) toward a diversified portfolio of EFV technologies.

The global policy landscape has intensified this transition. At the COP28 climate summit in 2023, numerous nations committed to phasing out new ICEV sales by 2035 or 2040 (UNFCCC, 2023). Complementing these international pledges, the European Union has implemented rigorous regulations effectively prohibiting the sale of new gasoline and diesel vehicles from 2035 (European Commission, 2023). These institutional frameworks underscore the strategic primacy of the EFV sector in contemporary industrial policy.

From an evolutionary economics perspective, extensive empirical literature suggests that the stringency of environmental regulations acts as a catalyst for "induced innovation" (Johnstone et al., 2010; Popp, 2019). Specifically, renewable energy mandates and stringent emission standards have been shown to significantly bolster patenting activities in clean vehicle technologies (Dechezleprêtre & Glachant, 2014). Furthermore, national strategic capacities and path dependencies shape the divergent trajectories of the electric vehicle (EV) industry, as nations leverage their specific industrial strengths and policy priorities (Meckling & Nahm, 2018).

H. Fujii, *Key Drivers of Environmental Innovation*,
https://doi.org/10.1007/978-981-92-0060-3_4

The market dynamics of EFVs reflect this rapid technological evolution. The IEA's Global Electric Vehicle Outlook 2024 reports that EV sales reached 14 million units in 2023—a 35% year-on-year increase—accounting for approximately 18% of global new vehicle registrations (IEA, 2024b). While projections suggest EVs could exceed one-third of the market by 2030, achieving net-zero targets requires further acceleration in charging infrastructure deployment, battery density improvements, and cost reduction. In this transition, hybrid technologies remain a pragmatic bridge for regions with infrastructure deficits, while hydrogen fuel cell technologies offer a promising decarbonization pathway for the heavy-duty and commercial sectors.

Beyond climate mitigation, the adoption of EFV technology addresses critical socio-economic externalities. It facilitates the improvement of urban air quality—an urgent public health priority in rapidly motorizing emerging economies like China and India—enhances energy security by reducing petroleum dependency, and fosters new industrial clusters. Against this backdrop, this chapter investigates the R&D dynamics and dissemination patterns of EFV technologies. By utilizing patent data as a high-fidelity proxy for technological effort and direction, I analyze how global R&D priorities have shifted and how different national innovation systems respond to the dual imperatives of environmental sustainability and industrial competitiveness.

4.1.2 Literature Review: Patent Analysis in EFV Technology

In evaluating the evolution of EFV technologies, patent data serve as a robust proxy for technological innovation. Patent information facilitates not only a quantitative assessment of R&D intensity but also a multifaceted analysis of technological maturity, international comparative advantage, and patterns of knowledge diffusion. Given the automotive industry's high propensity to patent, such data are indispensable for decoding corporate strategic positioning and the shifting landscape of industrial competitiveness during the green transition. This section systematically reviews the extant academic literature, organizing the major research trajectories in chronological order to highlight the evolution of the field.

Early empirical studies focused on identifying the fundamental drivers of environmental innovation. Oltra and Saint Jean (2009) analyzed major manufacturers from 1990 to 2005, identifying a triad of drivers: regulatory pressure, fuel price volatility, and internal technological capabilities. Their work was pioneering in distinguishing between general emission standards, which tend to promote incremental fuel efficiency improvements, and technology-forcing regulations—such as California's Zero Emission Vehicle (ZEV) mandate—which acted as a catalyst for radical innovation in electrification.

In the mid-2010s, the focus expanded to include market dynamics and the persistence of traditional technologies. Wesseling et al. (2014) examined the development cycles of Environmentally Friendly Vehicles (EFVs), arguing that technological investment by incumbents is often a strategic response to competitive threats from new entrants. Concurrently, Bergek and Berggren (2014) underscored that despite the push for radical shifts, incremental innovation in internal combustion engine (ICEV) efficiency—such as direct injection and variable valve timing—remained a dominant and sophisticated field of R&D, with distinct regional specializations. Building on this line of inquiry, Wesseling et al. (2015) analyzed patent portfolios to show how corporate heterogeneity and the choice between "niche" versus "multi-path" exploratory strategies determined the success of technological transitions, noting the early strategic dominance of Japanese manufacturers in hybrid technologies.

A significant theoretical and empirical advancement was marked by Aghion et al. (2016), who provided seminal evidence on directed technical change. Their study demonstrated that market-based instruments, such as carbon taxes and fuel prices, induce firms to pivot their innovative efforts from "dirty" to "clean" technologies. By analyzing firm-level data over several decades, they identified a profound path dependence: a firm's innovation trajectory is heavily influenced by its own R&D history and aggregate knowledge spillovers. This finding crystallized the understanding that proactive policy intervention is essential to overcome technological lock-in.

Building on these foundations and moving into the current decade, Zhang and Fujii (2025) introduced a highly granular analytical framework using the Logarithmic Mean Divisia Index (LMDI) decomposition. By analyzing patenting activities across the five major patent offices (CNIPA, USPTO, EPO, JPO, and KIPO), they decomposed patent growth into scale effects, structural shifts, and technology-specific priorities. This methodology allows for a rigorous comparison of how national innovation systems respond differently to policy incentives in an increasingly globalized R&D environment. The analytical framework employed in this chapter extends the LMDI decomposition approach used in their earlier study, applying it to a broader temporal scope and integrating it with comparative analysis across the IP5 patent offices over three decades.

In summary, the extant literature utilizing patent data to analyze EFVs yields a cohesive understanding of the sector's evolution, which can be synthesized into three overarching dimensions.

First, the landscape of international competitiveness has transitioned into a complex multipolar structure. While Japan maintains a clear technological leadership in hybrid and hydrogen fuel cell systems, China has rapidly redefined the market through a massive quantitative surge in electric vehicle (EV) patents. Meanwhile, the United States and Europe continue to exert influence by maintaining qualitative superiority in foundational areas such as battery chemistry and sophisticated electronic control systems.

This competitive dynamics is closely intertwined with the divergent technological life cycles of EFVs. The industry does not move in a single monolithic wave; rather, hybrid technology is increasingly characterized as reaching a mature phase, whereas EV technology remains in a high-growth trajectory. Hydrogen fuel cells, by contrast, are still navigating a nascent introduction phase. To capture these nuances, recent scholarly efforts have increasingly adopted advanced computational techniques, such as machine learning and text mining, to detect emerging technology convergences and disruptive shifts that traditional patent classifications might overlook.

Ultimately, the trajectory of these technologies underscores the profound efficacy of policy instruments in steering private-sector innovation. There is a robust academic consensus that regulatory frameworks—ranging from stringent fuel economy standards to New Energy Vehicle (NEV) quotas—effectively "pull" technological development by reducing market uncertainty. The strong geographic correlation between specific legal mandates, such as those implemented in California and China, and the subsequent localized surges in patenting activity provides compelling empirical evidence of the power of institutional frameworks in shaping the global future of sustainable mobility.

4.1.3 Global Trends in EFV Technology Patent Applications

Patent data serve as a critical diagnostic tool for evaluating the development of EFV technology, providing empirical evidence of innovation patterns and shifting technological trajectories (Haščič & Migotto, 2015). In the automotive sector, characterized by R&D-intensive competition, firms leverage the legal exclusivity of patents to recoup substantial investments and signal their technological prowess. As the industry pivots toward sustainable mobility, the strategic accumulation of patent portfolios in electric, hybrid, and hydrogen fuel cell domains has become a definitive indicator of a firm's future market competitiveness and strategic positioning.

According to global data from the World Intellectual Property Organization (WIPO) and major national patent offices, the volume of EFV-related patent applications has expanded markedly since the mid-2000s (WIPO, 2024). This growth reflects a significant qualitative shift: while the early 2000s were dominated by incremental improvements in internal combustion engine (ICEV) efficiency and hybrid vehicle (HV) systems, the 2010s witnessed a surge in electric vehicle (EV) technologies.

The acceleration of EFV patenting since 2010, as illustrated in Fig. 4.1, reflects a convergence of technology-forcing regulations, fiscal incentives (such as purchase subsidies), and a shift in consumer preferences. Notably, the period between 2008 and 2012 shows a distinct spike in activity. This trend coincides with the global economic stimulus measures following the 2008 financial crisis, during which major economies prioritized "green recovery" as a core industrial strategy. While the total number of applications peaked around 2011 followed by a brief stabilization, momentum was regained after 2017, predominantly driven by the exponential growth in EV technologies.

The transformation of the technological landscape is even more evident in the relative shares shown in Fig. 4.2. In the early 2000s, ICEV and HV technologies collectively accounted for approximately 80% of the patenting landscape, reflecting the market introduction phase of pioneers like the Toyota Prius. However, by around 2015, EV technology became the dominant field, exceeding 40% of the total share. This shift was fueled by the maturation of lithium-ion technology and the global expansion of charging networks. Conversely, the share of ICEV patents has continuously dwindled, dropping to the 20% range by 2020. This trend underscores the

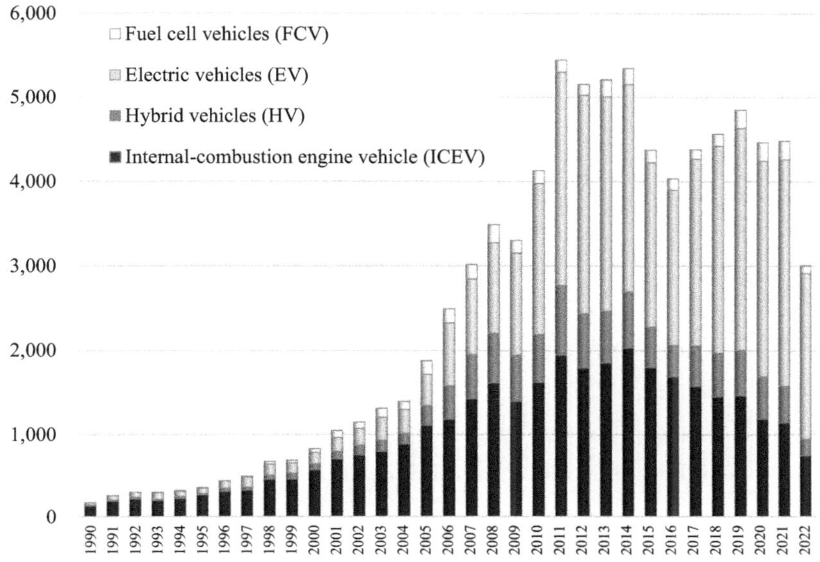

Fig. 4.1 Number of patent applications related to EFV technology in the patent cooperation treaty. *Note* While the 2022 figures in the current dataset show a nominal decline, this often reflects the conventional 18-month publication lag in patent filings rather than a reduction in actual R&D effort. *Source* OECD, STI Microdata Lab: Intellectual Property Database, http://oe.cd/ipstats, created by the author

diminishing marginal returns of traditional powertrain R&D and a decisive shift in the technological paradigm.

Furthermore, while HV technology peaked in 2011 and has since stabilized, it increasingly appears to serve as a bridge technology. Hydrogen fuel cell (FCV) technology, despite maintaining a smaller niche of less than 10%, has shown renewed vitality since 2020, likely reflecting the emergence of national hydrogen strategies aimed at decarbonizing heavy-duty transport.

In conclusion, the dual evidence of absolute growth (Fig. 4.1) and structural reallocation (Fig. 4.2) confirms a fundamental transformation in the automotive industry. R&D resources are being massively redirected from internal combustion toward electrification, vividly illustrating the new frontiers of global industrial competitiveness.

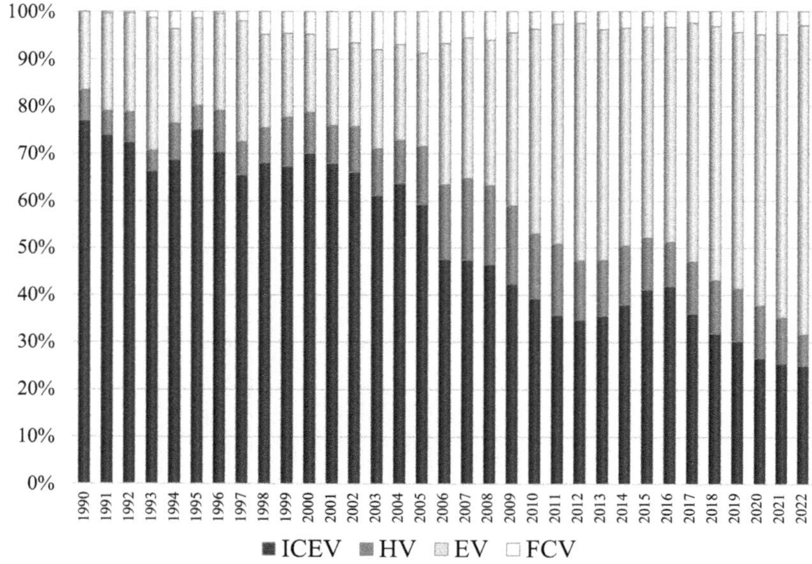

Fig. 4.2 Share of patent applications related to EFV technology in the patent cooperation treaty. *Source* OECD, STI Microdata Lab: Intellectual Property Database, http://oe.cd/ipstats, created by the author

4.2 Data and Methodology

4.2.1 EFV Technology Patent Data

Analysis using the International Patent Classification (IPC) categorizes EFV technology into five major technology fields: conventional vehicles (ICEV), hybrid vehicles (HV), electric vehicles (EV), fuel efficiency-improving design (EFFICIENCY), and fuel cell vehicles (FCV). Table 4.1 defines these fields using the IPC codes established by the OECD for climate change mitigation technologies in transport.

As summarized in Table 4.2, there are significant differences in the total volume and technological composition of EFV patents across the major patent offices (IP5). The China National Intellectual Property Administration (CNIPA) holds the largest cumulative volume at 192,962 applications, characterized by a dominant focus on EVs (50% share). It is followed by the Japan Patent Office (JPO) at 158,779, which maintains a unique strength in hybrid technology (15% share, the highest among IP5). The United States Patent and Trademark Office (USPTO) recorded 144,088 applications, while the European Patent Office (EPO) and the Korean Intellectual Property Office (KIPO) recorded 70,668 and 55,674 applications, respectively.

The massive volume at CNIPA reflects China's strategic shift toward New Energy Vehicles (NEVs). Since 2009, aggressive purchase subsidies and R&D incentives have stimulated a surge in patenting, particularly in battery electric vehicles. In

Table 4.1 Technology fields of EFV technology

Group	Technology	Definition (IPC code)
ICEV	Conventional vehicles (based on internal combustion engine vehicle: ICEV)	Y02T10/10-40
HV	Hybrid vehicles	Y02T10/62
EV	Electric vehicles	Y02T10/64-72
EFFICIENCY	Fuel efficiency-improving vehicle design (common to all road vehicles)	Y02T10/80-92
FCV	Application of hydrogen technology to transportation, e.g., using fuel cells	Y02T90/40

Source OECD, STI Microdata Lab: Intellectual Property Database, http://oe.cd/ipstats, created by the author https://stats.oecd.org/wbos/fileview2.aspx?IDFile=c5c477c0-d300-42fe-af1f-d4a450c79a39

Table 4.2 Number of EFV technology patent applications from 1990 to 2022

Patent office	Type	Total	ICEV	Hybrid	EV	FCV
CNIPA	Patent	192,962	73,332	16,643	97,266	5721
	Share	100%	38%	9%	50%	3%
USPTO	Patent	144,088	60,583	18,226	58,118	7161
	Share	100%	42%	13%	40%	5%
EPO	Patent	70,668	32,082	7950	27,905	2731
	Share	100%	45%	11%	39%	4%
JPO	Patent	158,779	72,023	24,044	58,307	4405
	Share	100%	45%	15%	37%	3%
KIPO	Patent	55,674	23,795	4438	24,690	2751
	Share	100%	43%	8%	44%	5%

Note Share represents the percentage of patent applications for each technology of total EFV technology
Source OECD, STI Microdata Lab: Intellectual Property Database, http://oe.cd/ipstats, created by the author

contrast, JPO's figures reflect Japan's early-mover advantage in hybrid systems, dating back to the launch of the Toyota Prius in 1997. Japanese firms have established an extensive portfolio covering regenerative braking and motor control systems.

The USPTO volume highlights a diversified innovation landscape, accelerated by post-2008 environmental regulations and the rise of EV specialists like Tesla. The EPO's relatively smaller volume is indicative of its stringent examination standards, where patents often represent high-quality, high-value inventions. KIPO's data, while the smallest in absolute terms, showcases South Korea's specialized competitive edge in battery technology and EV systems through its major industrial groups.

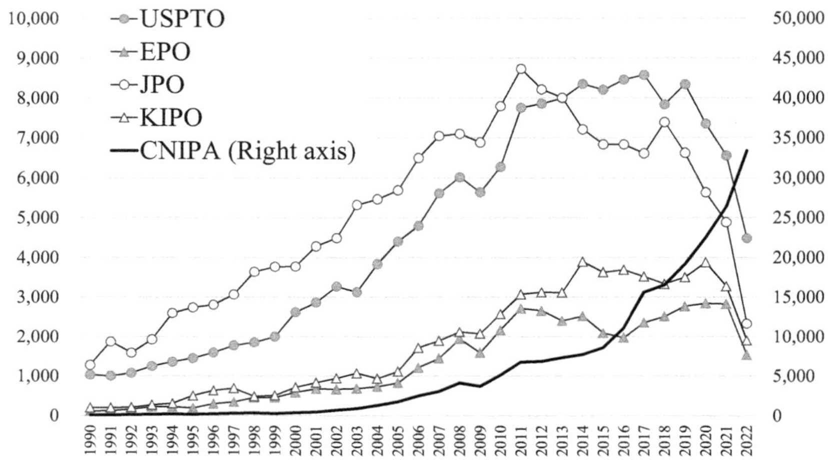

Fig. 4.3 Number of patent applications related to EFV technology in IP5. *Source* OECD, STI Microdata Lab: Intellectual Property Database, http://oe.cd/ipstats, created by the author

An analysis of annual trends reveals a stark divergence between China and other regions, as shown in Fig. 4.3. Consistent with the cross-sectoral pattern identified in the renewable energy domain (Chap. 3), the USPTO, EPO, JPO, and KIPO experienced a significant peak in EFV patent applications between 2008 and 2012, driven by post-crisis green stimulus packages and tightening emission standards, followed by a phase of stagnation or decline. In the EFV sector specifically, this trend was further reinforced by the consolidation of powertrain technology platforms and the plateauing of incremental fuel efficiency improvements in conventional vehicles. For instance, the JPO peaked at 8,729 applications in 2011 before receding to 4,884 in 2021.

Conversely, CNIPA continued its cross-sectoral exponential growth trajectory (see Chap. 3 for broader policy drivers), with EFV-specific applications surging to 26,363 in 2021 and further to 33,391 in 2022. In the EFV domain, this growth was particularly catalyzed by NEV-specific policies, including the dual-credit regulation system introduced in 2017, provincial-level EV production incentives, and the aggressive expansion of domestic battery manufacturing capacity led by firms such as CATL and BYD.

4.2.2 Comparative Analysis of EFV Technology Field Shares

The longitudinal shifts in technology field shares, as illustrated in Fig. 4.4, provide systematic evidence of evolving strategic priorities in EFV technology development. Across all patent offices, a universal expansion in the relative share of electric vehicle (EV) technology reflects a fundamental pivot in global R&D. The most aggressive transition occurred at the EPO, KIPO, and USPTO, where EV patent shares surged from 24–28% in the 2000s to a dominant level of 60% or higher by the 2020s. While CNIPA and JPO started from a slightly higher baseline (27–32%), their growth followed a similarly robust trajectory, with EV technologies accounting for more than half of their portfolios by the 2020s. This convergence is underpinned by three factors: technological breakthroughs in lithium-ion batteries and peripheral systems (BMS, thermal management); market infrastructure expansion reducing range anxiety; and decisive policy mandates, such as the EU's 2035 ban on ICEV sales and China's NEV credit system.

In contrast, the share of conventional internal combustion engine (ICEV) efficiency technologies has universally declined, though regional strategies remain divergent. The contraction was most severe at the EPO and KIPO, where shares plummeted from nearly 60% to approximately 24%. However, ICEV technology has not been abandoned; rather, it is being refined for the long-term transition period. Notably, at CNIPA, the ICEV share remained resilient at approximately 40% in the 2020s, while the JPO continues to pursue ultra-high-efficiency engines exceeding 50% thermal efficiency. These trends reflect a pragmatic recognition that improving the environmental performance of ICEVs remains critical as full electrification scales globally.

The trajectory of hybrid vehicle (HV) technology further underscores regional path dependencies. In Japan (JPO), the HV share remained remarkably resilient at 14–17%, signaling a persistent competitive advantage in refined powertrain systems. Conversely, the United States (USPTO) and Europe (EPO) exhibit a gradual contraction toward a 10% threshold as their systems pivot toward pure electrification. This divergence is most striking in China (CNIPA), where the HV share plummeted to a

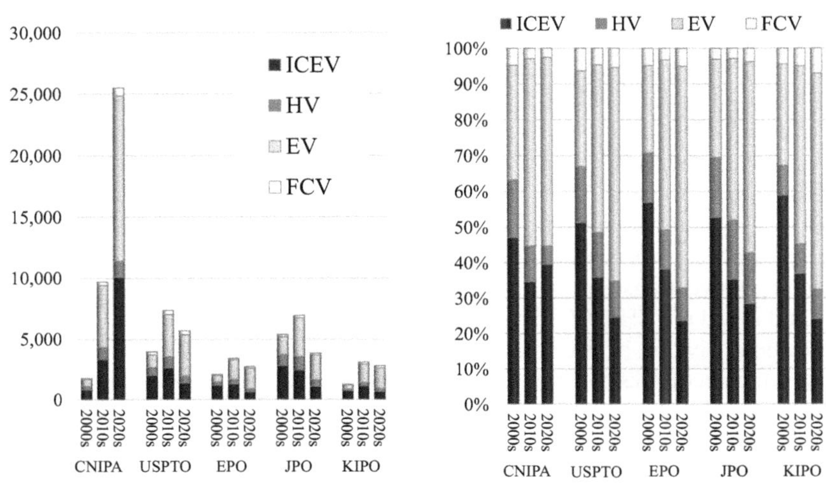

Fig. 4.4 Number and share of patent applications related to four types of EFV technologies. *Source* OECD, STI Microdata Lab: Intellectual Property Database, http://oe.cd/ipstats, created by the author

marginal 5%, reflecting a deliberate "leapfrogging" strategy that bypasses hybrids in favor of direct battery electrification.

Meanwhile, hydrogen fuel cell (FCV) technology demonstrates strategic persistence as a specialized solution for heavy-duty and commercial transport. In South Korea (KIPO), the FCV share showed a unique upward trend (5% to 7%), while the U.S. and Japan maintained stable shares of 4–6%. This persistence indicates that FCVs remain a vital long-term component in sectors where battery electrification faces inherent limitations.

Collectively, these patterns illustrate that the global transition to sustainable mobility is not following a singular technological path. Instead, it is progressing through a sophisticated mix of options—centered on pure electrification but complemented by ICEV refinement, hybrid persistence, and hydrogen systems—each strategically adapted to specific regional industrial strengths and institutional frameworks.

4.2.3 Patent Decomposition Analysis of EFV Technology

To evaluate the dynamic shifts in research and development, this section applies a factor decomposition framework to isolate the primary drivers of innovation in environmentally friendly vehicle (EFV) technologies. This approach builds upon the analytical concepts of patent decomposition introduced in Chap. 2, utilizing the LMDI methodology to provide a granular analysis of how these technologies have evolved alongside global regulatory changes. The LMDI method offers several theoretical advantages (Ang, 2005), including perfect decomposition without residual terms, consistency in aggregation across different levels of analysis, and symmetric treatment of positive and negative changes. The following four indicators are utilized to quantify EFV technological transitions:

I define the PRIORITY indicator as the number of specific EFV (e.g., electric vehicle) patent applications divided by the total number of EFV patent applications, thus providing the share of specific EFV patent applications among total EFV patents. This indicator increases if the number of specific EFV patent applications increases more quickly than the total number of EFV patent applications does, which indicates that inventors are concentrating their research resources on specific types of EFV technology inventions.

Similarly, the VEHICLE indicator is defined as the total number of EFV patent applications divided by the total number of environmental-related patent applications, which indicates the share of total EFV patents of all environmental technology patents. This indicator increases if the number of total EFV patent applications increases more quickly than the number of total environmental-related patent applications does, which indicates that inventors are concentrating their research resources on EFV technology more than on other environmental technology.

Next, ENVIRONMENT is defined as the relative importance of environmental-related technology among the total number of patent inventions. This indicator increases if the number of environmental-related technology patent applications increases more quickly than the total number of patent applications does. It shows how patent applicants are changing the priority of technological importance for environmental-related technologies relative to the patent as a whole.

Finally, the SCALE indicator is defined as the total number of patent applications and thus represents the scale of national research and development (R&D) activity. This indicator is affected by macro factors such as environmental policies, resource price fluctuations, and economic conditions.

Here, I introduce a decomposition approach using the electric vehicle (EV) technology group as a specific type of EFV patent application (Table 4.1). The number of EV technology patent applications ($\text{PATENT}_{\text{EV}}$) is decomposed using the total number of EFV technology patent applications ($\text{PATENT}_{\text{VEHICLE}}$), the total number of environmental-related patent applications ($\text{PATENT}_{\text{ENV}}$), and the total number of patent applications ($\text{PATENT}_{\text{TOTAL}}$), as shown in Eq. (4.1).

$$\begin{aligned} PATENT_{EV} &= \frac{PATENT_{EV}}{PATENT_{VEHICLE}} \times \frac{PATENT_{VEHICLE}}{PATENT_{ENV}} \\ &\times \frac{PATENT_{ENV}}{PATENT_{TOTAL}} \times PATENT_{TOTAL} \\ &= PRIORITY \times VEHICLE \times ENVIRONMENT \times SCALE \end{aligned} \tag{4.1}$$

I consider the change in EV technology patent applications from year t ($PATENT_{EV}^{t}$) to year $t+1$ ($PATENT_{EV}^{t+1}$). Using Eq. (4.1), the change in EV vehicle technology patent applications can be represented as follows.

$$\begin{aligned} \frac{PATENT_{EV}^{t+1}}{PATENT_{EV}^{t}} &= \frac{PRIORITY^{t+1}}{PRIORITY^{t}} \times \frac{VEHICLE^{t+1}}{VEHICLE^{t}} \\ &\times \frac{ENVIRONMENT^{t+1}}{ENVIRONMENT^{t}} \times \frac{SCALE^{t+1}}{SCALE^{t}} \end{aligned} \tag{4.2}$$

I can transform Eq. (4.2) into a natural logarithmic function and thus obtain Eq. (4.3).

$$\begin{aligned} \ln\left(PATENT_{EV}^{t+1}\right) - \ln\left(PATENT_{EV}^{t}\right) &= \ln\left(\frac{PRIORITY^{t+1}}{PRIORITY^{t}}\right) + \ln\left(\frac{VEHICLE^{t+1}}{VEHICLE^{t}}\right) \\ &+ \ln\left(\frac{ENVIRONMENT^{t+1}}{ENVIRONMENT^{t}}\right) + \ln\left(\frac{SCALE^{t+1}}{SCALE^{t}}\right) \end{aligned} \tag{4.3}$$

Multiplying both sides of Eq. (4.3) by $\omega_t^{(t+1)} = (\text{PATENT}_{EV}^{(t+1)} - \text{PATENT}_{EV}^{t})/\{\ln(\text{PATENT}_{EV}^{(t+1)}) - \ln(\text{PATENT}_{EV}^{t})\}$ yields Eq. (4.4) as follows.

$$\text{PATENT}_{EV}^{t+1} - \text{PATENT}_{EV}^{t} = \triangle\ \text{PATENT}_{EV}^{t,t+1}$$

$$= \omega_t^{t+1}\ln\left(\frac{\text{PRIORITY}^{t+1}}{\text{PRIORITY}^t}\right) + \omega_t^{t+1}\ln\left(\frac{\text{VEHICLE}^{t+1}}{\text{VEHICLE}^t}\right) + \omega_t^{t+1}\ln\left(\frac{\text{ENVIRONMENT}^{t+1}}{ENVIRONMENT^t}\right) + \omega_t^{t+1}\ln\left(\frac{\text{SCALE}^{t+1}}{\text{SCALE}^t}\right) \quad (4.4)$$

Therefore, changes in the number of patent applications for EV technologies ($\text{PATENT}_{\text{EV}}$) are decomposed based on changes in PRIORITY (first term), VEHICLE (second term), ENVIRONMENT (third term), and SCALE (fourth term).

4.3 Results of the Patent Decomposition Analysis

Figures 4.5, 4.6, 4.7, 4.8, and 4.9 show the cumulative changes in EFV technology patent applications calculated using the LMDI-based patent decomposition analysis. Following the same analytical framework as in Chap. 3, the plotted red dots show the estimated change in patent applications relative to the 2000s baseline, and the bar charts show the contribution of each determinant. The values are based on the total number of patent applications in each period, with the 2000s (2000–2009), 2010s (2010–2019), and 2020s (2020–2022) defined as in Chap. 3.

As in Chap. 3, where the analysis focused on the two dominant technologies (wind and solar power) within renewable energy, this chapter focuses on ICEVs and EVs, the two technologies that account for the majority of patents in EFV technology. The results of each analysis are shown in Figs. 4.5, 4.6, 4.7, 4.8, and 4.9. Each figure shows the factors affecting changes in the number of patent applications for ICEV technology on the left and for EV technology on the right.

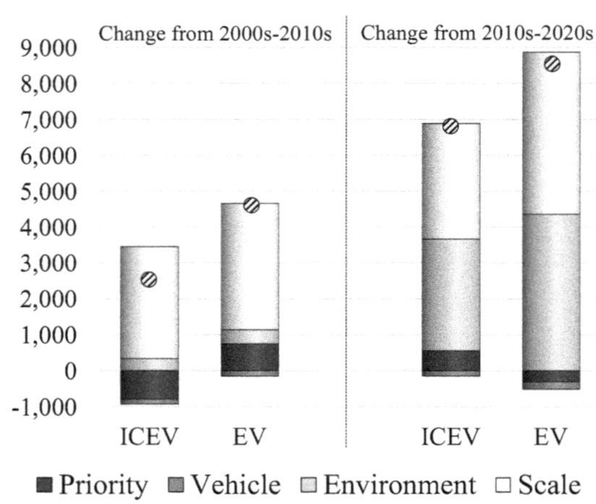

Fig. 4.5 Results of the patent decomposition analysis for the CNIPA. *Note* The y-axis is standardized such that the number of patent changes in the first year of each period is zero. The sum of the bars equals the value of the plotted points

4.3.1 *Results of the Patent Decomposition Analysis for the CNIPA*

As shown in Fig. 4.5, the number of patent applications for internal combustion engine (ICE) fuel efficiency improvement technologies and electric vehicle (EV) technologies in China increased significantly from the 2000s to the 2010s and again from the 2010s to the 2020s.

The factors driving the increase in ICEV technology patents differ between the two periods. In the 2000s–2010s period, the increase was driven predominantly by the SCALE effect. The ENVIRONMENT effect made a modest positive contribution, while the PRIORITY effect contributed negatively. In the 2010s–2020s period, both the SCALE effect and the ENVIRONMENT effect made substantial positive contributions of comparable magnitude, together accounting for the majority of the increase. The PRIORITY effect also turned positive, further reinforcing the growth. Across both periods, the value of the VEHICLE effect is small. This indicates that the proportion of EFV technology patents within the overall environmental patents has shown little change.

The shift in the PRIORITY effect from negative to positive is particularly noteworthy. The negative PRIORITY effect in the 2000s–2010s period suggests that fuel efficiency improvement technologies for internal combustion engines were not strategic priorities within China's EFV technology development strategy during the 2000s. Chinese companies focused on introducing and refining established technologies from Europe, the U.S., and Japan, prioritizing the practical application and mass production of existing technologies over creating innovative patents. The reversal to a positive PRIORITY effect in the 2010s–2020s period indicates that ICEV technology regained strategic importance, likely reflecting the re-evaluation of advanced engine technologies for use in hybrid vehicles.

The factor decomposition for EV technology reveals a contrasting pattern. In the 2000s–2010s period, the SCALE effect was the dominant driver, followed by a notable positive contribution from the PRIORITY effect, which indicates that EV technology was a clear strategic priority in this period. The ENVIRONMENT effect made a relatively modest contribution. In the 2010s–2020s period, the growth was driven by two dominant factors: the ENVIRONMENT effect and the SCALE effect. In contrast, the PRIORITY effect turned negative, and the VEHICLE effect remained small.

The PRIORITY effect for EV technology shows the opposite trend compared with that of ICEV technology: it was positive in the 2000s–2010s period but turned negative in the 2010s–2020s period. This reversal likely reflects a shift in strategic focus within the EFV technology domain. During the 2000s–2010s, China prioritized pure electric vehicle technology, directing concentrated investment into this area. However, by the 2010s–2020s, the strategic emphasis broadened as China experienced limitations in EV adoption, such as reduced performance in winter and uneven charging infrastructure. Consequently, in the 2020s, the relative priority of EV technology within the broader EFV portfolio slightly declined as resources were redirected toward advanced engines designed for plug-in hybrid electric vehicles (PHEVs), where the internal combustion engine was redefined not as "old technology" but as "a cutting-edge power generation unit complementing electric vehicles."

4.3.2 Results of the Patent Decomposition Analysis for the USPTO

As shown in Fig. 4.6, the number of patent applications for ICEVs (fuel efficiency improvement technologies for conventional internal combustion engine vehicles) and EVs (electric vehicle technology) in the United States shows a different trend from that of China. Namely, after increasing from the 2000s to the 2010s, these numbers decreased or showed little change from the 2010s to the 2020s. This trend reflects shifts in the priority of EFV technology development in the United States, changes in the market environment, and significant policy fluctuations accompanying administrative transitions.

The factors driving changes in ICEV technology patents differ markedly between the two periods. In the 2000s–2010s period, the increase was driven by the ENVIRONMENT effect, the SCALE effect, and the VEHICLE effect, all of which made positive contributions. Among these, the ENVIRONMENT effect was the largest contributor, followed by the SCALE effect and the VEHICLE effect. However, the PRIORITY effect was strongly negative, substantially offsetting the positive contributions of the other three factors. In the 2010s–2020s period, patent applications for ICEV technology declined. The PRIORITY effect remained strongly negative, the VEHICLE effect and the ENVIRONMENT effect also turned negative, and the

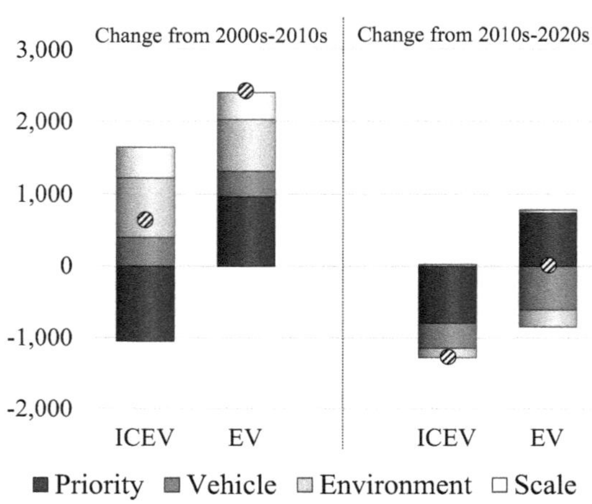

Fig. 4.6 Results of the patent decomposition analysis for the USPTO. *Note* The y-axis is standardized such that the number of patent changes in the first year of each period is zero. The sum of the bars equals the value of the plotted points

SCALE effect was close to zero. As a result, all factors contributed negatively or negligibly to the change, leading to an overall decrease in ICEV patent applications.

The consistently negative PRIORITY effect for ICEV technology across both periods is particularly noteworthy. In the 2000s–2010s period, this negative effect reflects the policy environment in the United States during the 2010s. The U.S. government introduced highly ambitious regulations, mandating an average fuel economy of 54.5 mpg (approximately 23.2 km/L) by 2025. Meeting this high threshold required more than minor engine refinements; manufacturers were compelled to shift a substantial portion of their research and development (R&D) expenditures toward electric drive (EV/PHEV) technologies, reducing the strategic priority of conventional ICEV improvement. The continued negative PRIORITY effect in the 2010s–2020s period indicates that this strategic de-prioritization of ICEV technology persisted, as the automotive industry's focus on electrification further intensified.

The factor decomposition for EV technology reveals a contrasting pattern. In the 2000s–2010s period, the PRIORITY effect was the dominant driver of patent growth, followed by the ENVIRONMENT effect, the SCALE effect, and the VEHICLE effect, all of which made positive contributions. The strong positive PRIORITY effect indicates that EV technology was a clear strategic priority in this period. In the 2010s–2020s period, however, the total number of EV patent applications showed almost no change. Although the PRIORITY effect remained positive, its contribution was largely offset by the strongly negative VEHICLE effect and the negative ENVIRONMENT effect. The SCALE effect was close to zero.

The strong positive PRIORITY effect for EV technology in the 2000s–2010s period can be attributed to active U.S. policy support during this decade. As noted in Chap. 3 (Sect. 3.5.2), the ARRA (American Recovery and Reinvestment Act) allocated approximately $90 billion to clean energy investment overall; of this, $2.5 billion was directly allocated to R&D for electric vehicles and battery technology. The Department of Energy provided low-interest loans to companies such as Tesla and Ford through the Advanced Technology Vehicle Manufacturing (ATVM) program. Furthermore, the federal government introduced a tax credit of up to $7500 for electric vehicle purchasers, and California's ZEV (Zero Emission Vehicle) regulations were significantly strengthened in 2012. These policies directed corporate R&D investment toward EV technology, resulting in a strong positive PRIORITY effect.

In the 2010s–2020s period, the PRIORITY effect for EV technology remained positive, suggesting that the strategic emphasis on EV technology within the EFV portfolio continued. However, the strongly negative VEHICLE effect indicates that the proportion of EFV technology patents within the broader environmental patent portfolio declined substantially. This decline likely reflects a combination of factors, including a broader diversification of environmental technology R&D beyond vehicle-related technologies and the policy uncertainty associated with administrative transitions. The ENVIRONMENT effect also turned negative, suggesting a relative decline in the overall environmental patent activity. As a result, despite the continued strategic prioritization of EV technology, the total number of EV patent applications in the United States remained nearly unchanged between the 2010s and the 2020s.

4.3.3 Results of the Patent Decomposition Analysis for the EPO

As shown in Fig. 4.7, the numbers of patent applications for internal combustion engine vehicles (ICEVs) and electric vehicles (EVs) in Europe exhibit trends similar to those observed in the United States. ICEV patent applications increased modestly from the 2000s to the 2010s but declined substantially from the 2010s to the 2020s. EV patent applications increased significantly from the 2000s to the 2010s but showed little change from the 2010s to the 2020s. These trends clearly reflect the structural transformation of the European automotive industry, driven by stricter environmental regulations and a strategic shift toward electrification.

The factors driving changes in ICEV technology patents differ between the two periods. In the 2000s–2010s period, the ENVIRONMENT effect was the largest positive contributor, followed by the SCALE effect and the VEHICLE effect. However, the PRIORITY effect was strongly negative, largely offsetting the positive contributions of the other three factors. As a result, the net increase in ICEV patent applications was modest. In the 2010s–2020s period, patent applications for ICEV technology declined substantially. The PRIORITY effect remained strongly negative, and the VEHICLE effect also turned negative. The ENVIRONMENT effect was close to zero, and the SCALE effect made only a small positive contribution. As a result, the negative effects dominated, leading to an overall decrease in ICEV patent applications.

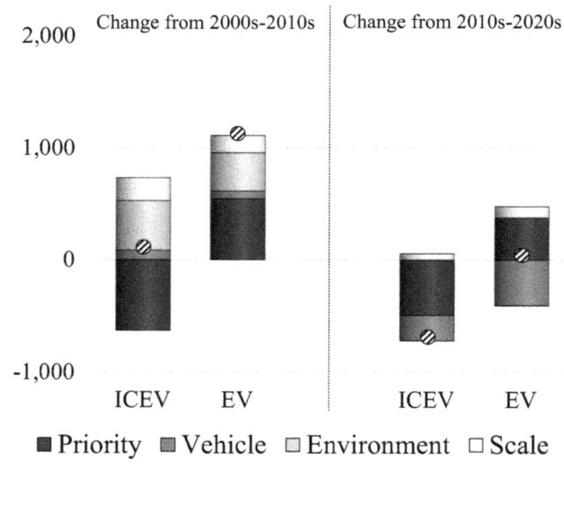

Fig. 4.7 Results of the patent decomposition analysis for the EPO. *Note* The y-axis is standardized such that the number of patent changes in the first year of each period is zero. The sum of the bars equals the value of the plotted points

The consistently negative PRIORITY effect for ICEV technology across both periods is particularly noteworthy. European manufacturers had previously centered their environmental strategy on "clean diesel," but this credibility collapsed following the emissions scandal in 2015. This event prompted European automakers to shift their R&D focus from internal combustion engines to EVs. Furthermore, the EU introduced the world's strictest CO_2 emissions regulations, providing a strong incentive for automakers to de-prioritize conventional ICEV improvement and redirect their R&D strategies toward EV development. The persistent negative PRIORITY effect in the 2010s–2020s period indicates that this strategic shift away from ICEV technology continued and intensified.

The factor decomposition for EV technology reveals a contrasting pattern. In the 2000s–2010s period, the PRIORITY effect was the dominant driver of patent growth, followed by the ENVIRONMENT effect, the SCALE effect, and the VEHICLE effect, all of which made positive contributions. The strong positive PRIORITY effect indicates that EV technology was a clear strategic priority in this period. In the 2010s–2020s period, however, the total number of EV patent applications showed almost no change. Although the PRIORITY effect remained positive, its contribution was largely offset by the strongly negative VEHICLE effect. The ENVIRONMENT effect was close to zero, and the SCALE effect made a modest positive contribution.

The strong positive PRIORITY effect for EV technology across both periods reflects the sustained strategic emphasis on electrification in Europe. The phased strengthening of emission regulations (Euro standards) and the EU's decision to effectively ban the sale of new gasoline and diesel cars from 2035 onward directed corporate R&D investment toward EV technology, resulting in a persistently positive PRIORITY effect. However, in the 2010s–2020s period, the strongly negative VEHICLE effect indicates that the proportion of EFV technology patents within the broader environmental patent portfolio declined substantially. This decline likely reflects the diversification of environmental technology R&D in Europe beyond vehicle-related technologies, particularly toward renewable energy (as discussed in Chap. 3), energy storage, and other decarbonization technologies. As a result, despite the continued strategic prioritization of EV technology, the total number of EV patent applications at the EPO remained nearly unchanged between the 2010s and the 2020s.

Overall, the decomposition results for Europe show a pattern strikingly similar to that of the United States: the PRIORITY effect is consistently negative for ICEV technology and consistently positive for EV technology across both periods, indicating a clear and sustained strategic shift from ICEV to EV. However, a notable difference lies in the underlying drivers of this shift. While the U.S. shift was driven in part by market forces, such as the emergence of Tesla, and policy support through direct subsidies and tax credits, the European shift was driven primarily by regulatory pressure, including the emissions scandal and the EU's stringent CO_2 emissions regulations.

4.3.4 Results of the Patent Decomposition Analysis for the JPO

As shown in Fig. 4.8, the trends in patent applications for internal combustion engine vehicles (ICEVs) and electric vehicles (EVs) in Japan exhibit characteristics distinct from those of other major patent offices. ICEV patent applications declined in both periods, while EV patent applications rose from the 2000s to the 2010s but then fell from the 2010s to the 2020s. As in the renewable energy analysis (Chap. 3, Sect. 3.5.4), a distinguishing feature of Japan is that the SCALE effect was consistently negative across all periods and technologies, reflecting the prolonged economic stagnation and reduced corporate R&D expenditure that characterized the Japanese economy during these decades.

Turning to the decomposition of ICEV technology, the 2000s–2010s period presents a complex picture. The ENVIRONMENT effect and the VEHICLE effect both made substantial positive contributions, while the PRIORITY effect had a large negative impact and the SCALE effect was also negative. The positive contributions from the ENVIRONMENT and VEHICLE effects were largely offset by the negative PRIORITY and SCALE effects, resulting in a modest overall decline in ICEV patent applications. In the 2010s–2020s period, the decline in ICEV patents accelerated. The VEHICLE effect turned sharply negative and became the largest contributor to the decline, followed by the PRIORITY effect and the SCALE effect, all of which were negative. Only the ENVIRONMENT effect remained positive, though its magnitude was insufficient to counterbalance the negative contributions.

The positive ENVIRONMENT and VEHICLE effects observed in the 2000s–2010s period can be attributed to the Japanese government's introduction of the "next-generation vehicle" concept and its adoption of policies comprehensively

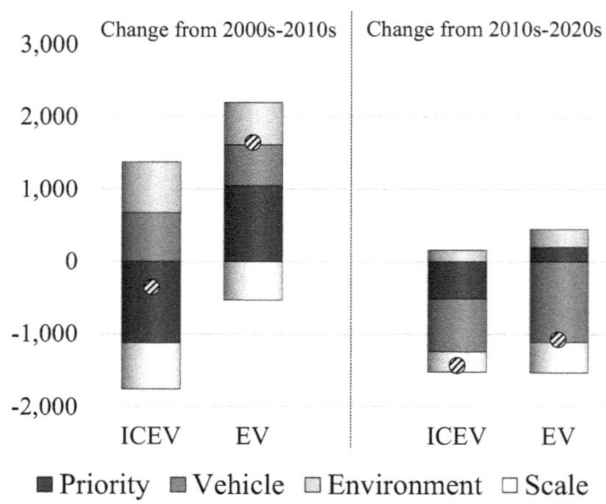

Fig. 4.8 Results of the patent decomposition analysis for the JPO. *Note* The y-axis is standardized such that the number of patent changes in the first year of each period is zero. The sum of the bars equals the value of the plotted points

supporting hybrid vehicles, electric vehicles, plug-in hybrid vehicles, fuel cell vehicles, and clean diesel vehicles. These broad-based policies encouraged patent applications across all EFV technologies, including ICEV improvement. The negative PRIORITY effect, meanwhile, indicates that despite this favorable policy environment, the strategic emphasis within EFV technology was shifting away from conventional engine improvement toward electrification. The reversal of the VEHICLE effect from positive to strongly negative in the 2010s–2020s period suggests that the share of EFV technology patents within the broader environmental patent portfolio declined, likely as environmental R&D diversified into non-vehicle domains.

For EV technology, the 2000s–2010s period saw a substantial increase in patent applications. The PRIORITY effect was the dominant positive driver, followed by the ENVIRONMENT effect and the VEHICLE effect. The SCALE effect, however, was negative, partially offsetting the gains. The strong positive PRIORITY effect confirms that EV technology was a clear strategic priority for Japanese firms during this period. In the 2010s–2020s period, however, EV patent applications declined substantially. The VEHICLE effect became strongly negative and was the largest contributor to the decline. The SCALE effect was also negative. Although the PRIORITY effect and the ENVIRONMENT effect remained positive, their combined contributions were far smaller than the negative effects, resulting in an overall decrease.

The decline in EV patent applications from the 2010s to the 2020s distinguishes Japan from other major patent offices. While EV patents continued to grow in China and remained roughly stable in the United States and Europe during the same period, Japan experienced a notable reduction. This outcome can be attributed primarily to the large negative VEHICLE effect and the persistent negative SCALE effect. The negative SCALE effect, unique to Japan among the five patent offices, reflects the broader contraction of patent activity at the JPO. Combined with the decline in the share of EFV patents within the environmental patent portfolio (the negative VEHICLE effect), these structural factors outweighed the continued, albeit diminished, strategic prioritization of EV technology. It is worth noting that the PRIORITY effect, while positive in both periods, weakened considerably from the 2000s–2010s to the 2010s–2020s. This moderation likely reflects the portfolio strategy adopted by Japanese automakers, who continued to invest in hybrid, plug-in hybrid, and fuel cell technologies alongside pure EVs, rather than concentrating resources exclusively on EV development as seen in other regions.

4.3.5 Results of the Patent Decomposition Analysis for the KIPO

As shown in Fig. 4.9, the trends in patent applications for ICEVs and EVs in South Korea broadly resemble those observed in the United States and Europe. ICEV patent applications increased from the 2000s to the 2010s but declined from the 2010s to the 2020s. EV patent applications grew substantially from the 2000s to the 2010s

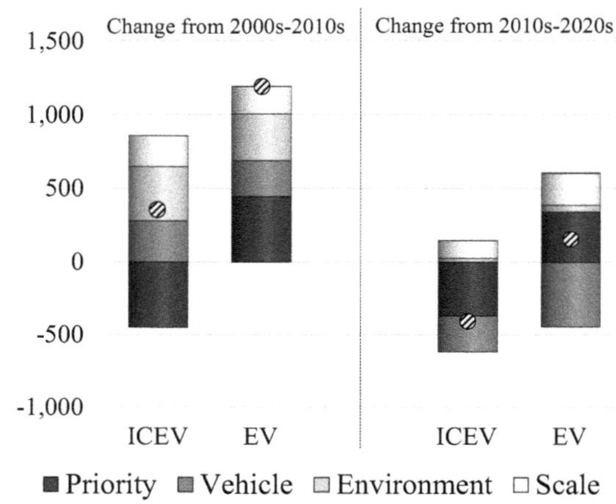

Fig. 4.9 Results of the patent decomposition analysis for the KIPO. *Note* The y-axis is standardized such that the number of patent changes in the first year of each period is zero. The sum of the bars equals the value of the plotted points

and continued to increase modestly from the 2010s to the 2020s. These trends reflect the bold electrification strategy of the Korean automotive industry and the global competitiveness of its battery sector.

The decomposition of ICEV technology patents reveals a clear two-phase pattern. In the 2000s–2010s period, the ENVIRONMENT effect was the largest positive contributor, followed by the VEHICLE effect and the SCALE effect. However, the PRIORITY effect was negative, partially offsetting the positive contributions. The net result was a moderate increase in ICEV patent applications. In the 2010s–2020s period, the trend reversed. The PRIORITY effect remained negative, and the VEHICLE effect also turned negative. Although the SCALE effect and the ENVIRONMENT effect were positive, their contributions were modest and insufficient to offset the negative effects. As a result, ICEV patent applications declined overall.

The consistently negative PRIORITY effect for ICEV technology across both periods reflects a deliberate strategic choice by Korean manufacturers. Unlike their Japanese counterparts, who maintained a diversified portfolio approach encompassing hybrid and other transitional technologies, Korean firms adopted a "leapfrog strategy" of direct transition from ICEVs to EVs. This strategic decision was driven by several factors: the recognition of Toyota's market dominance in hybrid technology and the need to circumvent existing patent barriers; Korea's competitive advantage in possessing world-class battery manufacturers such as LG Energy Solution, Samsung SDI, and SK On; and the strategic imperative that battery electric vehicle (BEV) technology is essential for competitiveness in the Chinese market.

The decomposition for EV technology presents a more uniformly positive picture in the 2000s–2010s period. All four factors—PRIORITY, ENVIRONMENT, VEHICLE, and SCALE—made positive contributions. Among these, the PRIORITY effect was the largest, underscoring the strong strategic emphasis on EV development. This broad-based positive pattern reflects the alignment of government policy, industry investment, and favorable structural conditions during this period. In 2009, the South Korean government announced its "Green Car Industry Development

Strategy," positioning hybrid vehicles, plug-in hybrid vehicles, electric vehicles, and fuel cell vehicles as next-generation vehicles, and introduced policies including R&D support, purchase subsidies, and tax incentives. In the 2010s–2020s period, the total number of EV patent applications continued to grow, though modestly. The PRIORITY effect and the SCALE effect remained positive, indicating sustained strategic emphasis and growing overall patent activity. However, the VEHICLE effect turned strongly negative, substantially offsetting the positive contributions. The ENVIRONMENT effect was small but positive.

The strongly negative VEHICLE effect in the 2010s–2020s period indicates that the proportion of EFV technology patents within the broader environmental patent portfolio declined. This pattern is consistent with that observed in the United States and Europe during the same period, suggesting a common trend of environmental R&D diversification beyond vehicle-related technologies. Nevertheless, the continued positive PRIORITY effect confirms that EV technology retained its position as a strategic priority for Korean firms.

4.4 Conclusion

In this chapter, I comprehensively analyzed patent trends for EFV technologies at the IP5 (United States Patent and Trademark Office, China National Intellectual Property Administration, European Patent Office, Japan Patent Office, and Korean Intellectual Property Office) from the 2000s to the 2020s. Using the LMDI decomposition method, we studied fuel efficiency improvement technologies for internal combustion engine vehicles (ICEVs) and electric vehicle (EV) technologies. The analysis reveals that the development priorities for EFVs vary significantly over time across countries and regions, with distinct patterns emerging based on specific industrial policies, market structures, technological maturity, and economic conditions.

The first major finding is the explosive growth in EFV technology patent applications in China and the evolving structure of contributing factors across periods. From the 2000s to the 2010s, the SCALE effect was the dominant driver, reflecting the overall expansion of patent application activity at the CNIPA. At the same time, the PRIORITY effect made a notable positive contribution to EV technology, indicating that electric vehicles were a clear strategic priority during this period. From the 2010s to the 2020s, the contributing factors shifted: the ENVIRONMENT effect and the SCALE effect became the two dominant drivers for both ICEV and EV technologies, while the PRIORITY effect reversed direction—turning positive for ICEV technology and negative for EV technology. This reversal suggests a broadening of China's EFV strategy, as the country re-evaluated the role of advanced internal combustion engines for use in plug-in hybrid vehicles alongside its continued expansion of pure electric vehicles.

The second key finding concerns the decline or stagnation in patent applications in the United States and Europe from the 2010s to the 2020s. In both regions, ICEV patent applications declined and EV patent applications showed little change during this period. A consistent pattern emerged in both regions: the PRIORITY effect was strongly negative for ICEV technology and positive for EV technology across both periods, demonstrating a clear and sustained strategic shift from ICEV to EV. However, the VEHICLE effect and the ENVIRONMENT effect turned negative in the 2010s–2020s period for both technologies, indicating that the proportion of EFV patents within the broader environmental patent portfolio declined and that overall environmental patent activity weakened. The underlying causes differ between the two regions. In the United States, policy uncertainty associated with administrative transitions and the increased economic appeal of fossil fuels due to the shale gas revolution diminished investment incentives for EFV technologies (see Chap. 3, Sect. 3.5.2, for a detailed discussion of the shale gas revolution and its impact on U.S. renewable energy innovation). In Europe, the 2015 Volkswagen emissions scandal (Dieselgate) led to a collapse in trust in diesel technology, accelerating the strategic shift from ICEV to EV, while the EU's stringent CO_2 emissions regulations provided further impetus for this transition.

The third finding highlights a clear divergence in the technology strategies of Japan and South Korea. A distinctive feature of Japan is that the SCALE effect was consistently negative across all periods and technologies, reflecting the overall contraction of patent application activity at the JPO. This stands in contrast to the other four patent offices. Furthermore, while the PRIORITY effect was positive for EV technology in both periods, it weakened considerably from the 2000s–2010s to the 2010s–2020s. This moderation reflects the "full lineup electrification strategy" adopted by Japanese automakers, who continued to invest across hybrid, plug-in hybrid, and fuel cell technologies alongside pure EVs, rather than concentrating resources exclusively on electric vehicle development. As a result, Japan was the only region among the IP5 where EV patent applications declined from the 2010s to the 2020s. In contrast, South Korea's decomposition results in the 2000s–2010s period showed positive contributions from all four factors for EV technology, reflecting a period of broad-based growth driven by aligned government policy and industry investment. The PRIORITY effect was consistently negative for ICEV technology and positive for EV technology across both periods, demonstrating a "leapfrog strategy" of direct transition from ICEVs to BEVs without relying on hybrid technology as an intermediate step. This strategic decision was supported by Korea's competitive advantage in battery manufacturing and the strategic imperative of competitiveness in the Chinese market.

In conclusion, patent trends in EFV technologies are shaped by the complex interplay of national industrial policies, market environments, technological maturity, and energy strategies. Decarbonizing the transportation sector is an urgent imperative for strengthening global climate action and achieving the Paris Agreement goals, making the development and adoption of EFV technologies critically important. The transition from ICEV to EV technology constitutes an irreversible trend, as evidenced by the consistently negative PRIORITY effect for ICEV technology and the positive PRIORITY effect for EV technology observed across most patent offices. However, the pace and pathway of this transition vary according to each country's circumstances. Nations must strengthen their strategic technological development investments based on their industrial bases, technological strengths, and market characteristics while simultaneously enhancing system-wide efforts such as charging infrastructure development, power grid integration, and adaptation to a circular economy. International cooperation, including standardization, technical collaboration, and ensuring a level playing field, is also essential. It is hoped that the findings of this research will contribute to decision-making by policymakers, researchers, and industry and accelerate the transition to sustainable mobility systems.

References

Aghion, P., Dechezleprêtre, A., Hémous, D., Martin, R., & Van Reenen, J. (2016). Carbon taxes, path dependency, and directed technical change: Evidence from the auto industry. *Journal of Political Economy, 124*(1), 1–51.

Ang, B. W. (2005). The LMDI approach to decomposition analysis: A practical guide. *Energy Policy, 33*(7), 867–871. https://doi.org/10.1016/j.enpol.2003.10.010

Bergek, A., & Berggren, C. (2014). The impact of environmental policy instruments on innovation: A review of energy and automotive industry studies. *Ecological Economics, 106,* 112–123.

Dechezleprêtre, A., & Glachant, M. (2014). Does foreign environmental policy influence domestic innovation? Evidence from the wind industry. *Environmental and Resource Economics, 58*(3), 391–413.

European Commission. (2023). *Commission welcomes completion of key 'Fit for 55' legislation, putting EU on track to exceed 2030 targets.* Brussels. https://ec.europa.eu/commission/presscorner/detail/en/ip_23_4754. Accessed on February 17, 2026.

Haščič, I., & Migotto, M. (2015). *Measuring environmental innovation using patent data* (OECD Environment Working Papers No. 89). OECD Publishing. https://doi.org/10.1787/5js009kf48xw-en.

International Energy Agency (IEA). (2024a). *World energy outlook 2024.* IEA. https://www.iea.org/reports/world-energy-outlook-2024

International Energy Agency (IEA). (2024b). *Global EV outlook 2024.* Paris. https://www.iea.org/reports/global-ev-outlook-2024

Johnstone, N., Haščič, I., & Popp, D. (2010). Renewable energy policies and technological innovation: Evidence based on patent counts. *Environmental and Resource Economics, 45*(1), 133–155.

Meckling, J., & Nahm, J. (2018). When do states disrupt industries? Electric vehicles and the politics of innovation. *Review of International Political Economy, 25*(4), 505–529.

Oltra, V., & Saint Jean, M. (2009). Variety of technological trajectories in low emission vehicles (LEVs): A patent data analysis. *Journal of Cleaner Production, 17*(2), 201–213.

Popp, D. (2019). Environmental policy and innovation: A decade of research. *International Review of Environmental and Resource Economics, 13*(3–4), 265–337.

United Nations Framework Convention on Climate Change (UNFCCC). (2023). *COP28 Dubai climate change conference.* UNFCCC. https://unfccc.int/cop28

Wesseling, J. H., Faber, J., & Hekkert, M. P. (2014). How competitive forces sustain electric vehicle development. *Technological Forecasting and Social Change, 81,* 154–164.

Wesseling, J. H., Niesten, E. M., Faber, J., & Hekkert, M. P. (2015). Business Strategies of Incumbents in the market for electric vehicles: Opportunities and incentives for sustainable innovation. *Business Strategy and the Environment, 24*(6), 518–531.

World Intellectual Property Organization (WIPO). (2024). *WIPO patent database.* WIPO. https://www.wipo.int/patentscope/en/

Zhang, Z., & Fujii, H. (2025). A global analysis of patent invention strategies in automotive technologies for environmental sustainability. *Sustainability, 17*(2), 696.

Chapter 5
Pollution Control Technology

5.1 Introduction

Pollution control technologies play a critical role in addressing environmental degradation and protecting public health. According to the World Health Organization (WHO), air pollution alone causes approximately 7 million premature deaths annually worldwide, making it one of the greatest environmental health risks (WHO, 2021). According to the Lancet Commission on pollution and health (Landrigan et al., 2022), pollution-related diseases account for 16% of all deaths globally, with the burden disproportionately affecting low- and middle-income countries.

Beyond health impacts, this challenge has economic and social dimensions. The World Bank (2016) estimates that air pollution costs the global economy more than 5 trillion US dollars annually in welfare costs, while inadequate water supply and sanitation impose approximately 260 billion US dollars in annual economic losses (World Bank, 2013). These figures underscore the urgency of developing and deploying effective solutions.

Patent data serve as a valuable indicator for assessing technological progress in this field. Patents provide quantifiable evidence of innovation, enabling the analysis of research and development (R&D) trends, technology maturity, and international competitiveness. According to OECD analysis, the number of environment-related patent applications has significantly increased since the 2000s, driven by policy incentives and regulatory pressures (Nesta et al., 2014), with such innovations representing a substantial portion of environmental advances (OECD, 2024).

Figure 5.1 presents the temporal evolution of patent applications filed through the Patent Cooperation Treaty (PCT) from 1990 to 2022, revealing several distinct phases in global innovation patterns. The period from 1990 to 2000 shows relatively modest but steady growth, with the total number of annual applications increasing from approximately 1,200 to 4,100. A notable acceleration began in the early 2000s, with total applications expanding rapidly to reach their peak of approximately 9200 in 2014. This growth trajectory reflects increasing environmental awareness globally

H. Fujii, *Key Drivers of Environmental Innovation*,
https://doi.org/10.1007/978-981-92-0060-3_5

and the emergence of stricter regulations in major economies (Johnstone et al., 2010; Popp, 2002). Following the mid-2010s peak, the total number of applications showed a gradual decline before stabilizing at approximately 8500–9200 annually during 2020–2022. This pattern suggests technological maturation in certain domains, particularly air pollution control, although innovation continues at substantial levels in other areas such as waste management.

Figure 5.2 illustrates the technology share composition within patent applications, highlighting the relative importance of different domains and notable shifts over time. Air pollution abatement has consistently been the largest category, accounting for approximately 40% of all applications in the early 1990s, rising to around 50% during the 2005–2015 period, before declining to nearly 37% by 2022. Water treatment technologies represent the second largest category, maintaining a relatively stable share of approximately 27–31% throughout the period. Waste management technologies, which accounted for approximately 20–26% of applications in the 1990s, experienced a relative decline to 18–20% during the 2005–2015 period, but have shown a notable resurgence in recent years, reaching 33% by 2022, surpassing their earlier shares. The residual category, which includes soil remediation and environmental monitoring technologies, consistently accounts for a small fraction of approximately 1–3% of total applications.

The evolving composition of technology shares reveals important structural shifts in innovation priorities. The declining share of air pollution abatement patents and the rising prominence of waste management technologies in recent years suggest a reorientation of R&D efforts, likely driven by growing policy attention to circular economy principles and sustainable waste processing (European Commission, 2019). Meanwhile, water treatment technologies have maintained steady innovation levels, reflecting the persistent and universal nature of water quality challenges across developed and developing economies.

The research, development, and diffusion of these technologies are examined in this chapter, and trends in technological development and changes in R&D priorities using patent information are explained. The analysis covers air pollution control, water treatment, and waste management as the three primary subcategories for decomposition analysis, with soil remediation and environmental monitoring grouped together as 'Others' due to their relatively small share of total applications (approximately 2%). By examining patent trends across major offices, including the China National Intellectual Property Administration (CNIPA), the United States Patent and Trademark Office (USPTO), the European Patent Office (EPO), the Japan Patent Office (JPO), and the Korean Intellectual Property Office (KIPO), this chapter provides insights into the global landscape of innovation in this field.

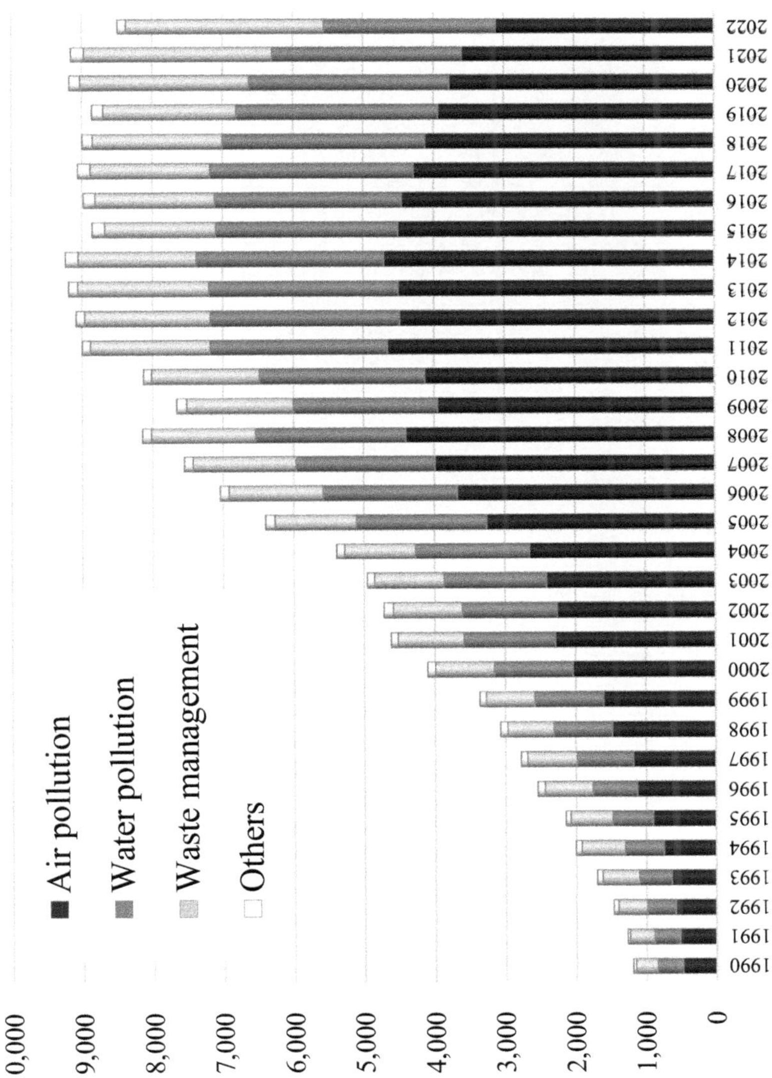

Fig. 5.1 Number of patent applications related to pollution control technology in the patent cooperation treaty. *Source* OECD, STI Microdata Lab: Intellectual Property Database, http://oe.cd/ipstats, created by the author

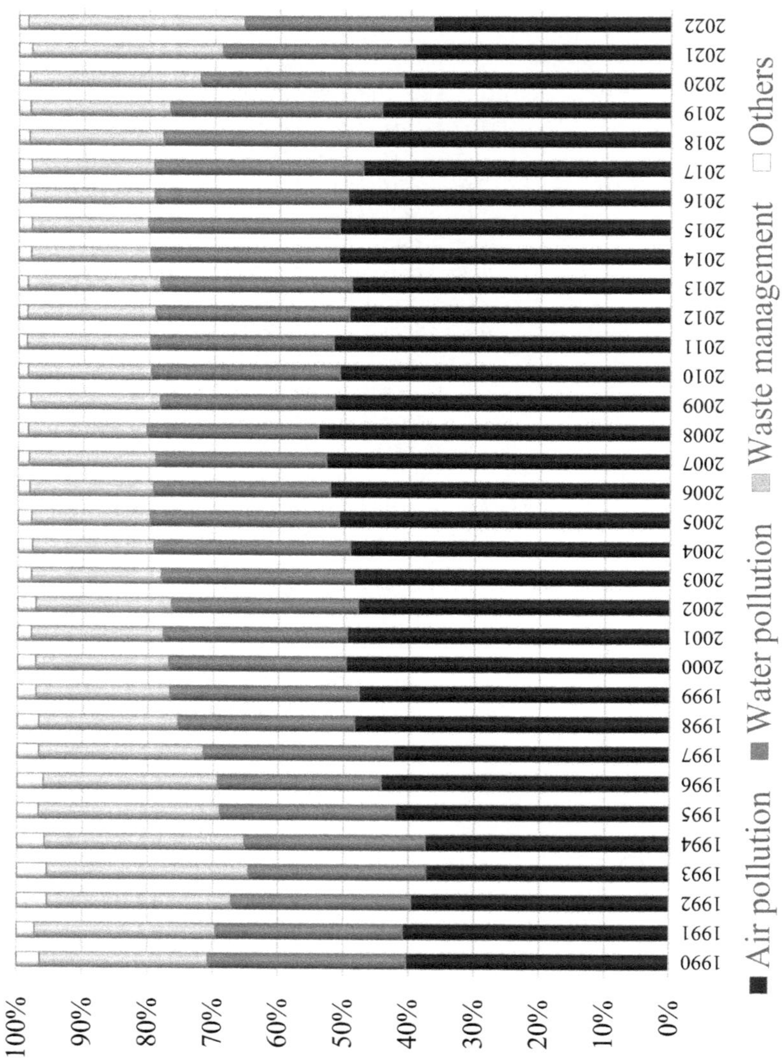

Fig. 5.2 Share of patent applications related to pollution control technology in the patent cooperation treaty. *Source* OECD, STI Microdata Lab: Intellectual Property Database, http://oe.cd/ipstats, created by the author

5.2 Literature Review: Patent Analysis in Pollution Control Technology

Patent data serve as a widely utilized indicator of technological innovation for evaluating progress in this field. Patent information enables not only quantitative assessment of R&D activity outcomes but also multifaceted analysis, including technology maturity, international competitiveness, and technology transfer patterns. This section systematically reviews academic research focusing on patent applications and grants, organizing major research trends and findings.

5.2.1 Air Pollution Control Technologies

Research in this domain focuses primarily on renewable energy and emission treatment technologies. Johnstone et al. (2010) empirically analyzed the impact of renewable energy policies on technological innovation using patent count data. Their study is significant for quantitatively demonstrating how policy incentives promote environmental technology innovation.

With respect to specific pollutant reduction technologies, Popp (2006) conducted an international comparative study on nitrogen oxide and sulfur oxide reduction using data from the United States, Japan, and Germany. The research revealed how environmental regulations in each country affect both domestic innovation and international technology diffusion, showing that stricter regulations promote local advancement while influencing cross-border technology transfer.

Lee et al. (2009) proposed a keyword-based patent mapping methodology aimed at systematically organizing technologies and discovering new approaches. This methodology visualizes relationships between technology domains through network analysis of keywords extracted from patent documents, thus enabling the discovery of new technological opportunities. Patent maps serve as valuable tools for formulating R&D strategies and optimizing technology portfolios.

Johnstone et al. (2017) investigate the relationships among environmental regulation, innovation, and competitiveness using environmental patent data. Covering thermal power plants in 20 countries from 1990–2009, the results show that regulatory stringency significantly improves the productive efficiency in terms of air pollutant emissions and fuel use but becomes negative beyond a certain threshold. Regulatory differentiation across plant size and age has negative effects that intensify over time. Finally, integrated environmental innovation approaches prove more effective for efficiency improvements than end-of-pipe technologies do.

5.2.2 Water Pollution Control Technologies

Research in this field has focused on membrane separation and other advanced treatment technologies. Daim et al. (2006) proposed an analytical approach that integrates patent and publication data for forecasting emerging technologies. Their study demonstrated that combining bibliometrics with patent analysis enables more accurate predictions of technology maturity and future development directions.

Kim and Lee (2015) conducted a comparative analysis of patent databases across countries, including water purification technologies. This study compared the characteristics of databases from the USPTO, EPO, JPO, and KIPO, clarifying the strengths and weaknesses of each for innovation research. Since database choice significantly affects analysis reliability and validity, such research provides important foundational information.

More recently, Mao et al. (2022) analyzed trends in industrial wastewater treatment and revealed development patterns of emerging approaches such as advanced oxidation processes (AOPs) and membrane technologies.

5.2.3 Waste Management Technologies

Waste management plays a central role in realizing a circular economy. Albino et al. (2014) clarified development trends in low-carbon technologies, including waste-to-energy, through patent analysis. Their study identified developmental stages through time series analysis and evaluated the growth rates and maturity levels of each domain. Waste-to-energy has attracted attention as an approach that simultaneously addresses waste disposal and energy challenges.

De Marchi (2012) empirically analyzed the relationship between environmental innovation and R&D cooperation in Spain's manufacturing sector. The research revealed that interfirm cooperation and industry–academia collaboration play important roles in environmental technology innovation, including waste treatment and recycling. Patent data were utilized to understand innovation network structures through the analysis of coapplication patterns.

Transitioning to a circular economy is essential for realizing a sustainable society. Ghisellini et al. (2016) comprehensively reviewed the role of waste technologies in this transition, organizing the current status and challenges from diverse information sources, including patent data. They indicated technological directions for the harmonious development of environmental and economic systems.

Recent research on the management and evaluation of circular economy patents has advanced significantly. Valero-Gil and Scarpellini (2024) proposed an analytical approach using the Y02W subcategory of the cooperative patent classification (CPC) for managing patents related to circular innovation.

5.3 Data and Methodology

5.3.1 Pollution Control Patent Data

This study categorizes pollution control technologies into four main groups using the International Patent Classification (IPC) codes defined by the OECD: (1) air pollution abatement technology (AIR), (2) water pollution abatement technology (WATER), (3) waste management technology (WASTE), and (4) other pollution control technology (OTHERS), which includes soil remediation and environmental monitoring. Table 5.1 shows the patent classification of pollution control technologies using the IPC codes as defined by the OECD.

5.3.2 Patent Decomposition Analysis of Pollution Control Technology

This section identifies the underlying forces shaping patenting activities by employing a comprehensive decomposition analysis of pollution control technologies. While Chap. 2 discusses the overarching significance and framework of patent data decomposition, this chapter operationalizes the LMDI method to analyze technologies addressing the multifaceted challenges of air, water, and waste management. To assess how R&D resources are strategically allocated across these technological domains, the following four indicators are developed:

PRIORITY Indicator: This indicator measures the share of specific pollution management (e.g., water treatment) patents of total pollution control patents. An increase indicates that inventors are concentrating research resources on particular technology types. POLLUTION Indicator: Defined as total pollution control patents divided by total environmental patents, this indicator reveals the relative focus on pollution control versus other environmental technologies. An increase suggests concentrated R&D effort in this field. ENVIRONMENT Indicator: This indicator captures the relative importance of environmental technologies among all patent inventions, indicating how applicants prioritize environmental innovations relative to overall patenting activity. SCALE Indicator: This indicator represents total patent applications, reflecting the scale of national R&D activity influenced by macro factors such as environmental policies, resource prices, and economic conditions.

Here, I introduce a decomposition approach using the water pollution abatement technology group as a specific type of pollution control application (Table 5.1). The number of water pollution abatement technology patent applications ($\mathrm{PATENT}_{\mathrm{WATER}}$) is decomposed using the total number of pollution control patent applications ($\mathrm{PATENT}_{\mathrm{POLLUTION}}$), the total number of environmental-related patent applications ($\mathrm{PATENT}_{\mathrm{ENV}}$), and the total number of patent applications ($\mathrm{PATENT}_{\mathrm{TOTAL}}$), as shown in Eq. (5.1).

Table 5.1 Groups of pollution control technologies

Group	Technology	Definition (IPC code)
Air pollution management	Emissions abatement from stationary sources (e.g., SOx, NOx, PM emissions from combustion plants)	B01D53/34-965, F23G7/06, F23J15, F27B1/18, C21B7/22, C21C5/38, F23B80, F23C9, F23C10
	Emissions abatement from mobile sources (e.g., NOx, CO, HC, PM emissions from motor vehicles)	B01D53/92, B01D53/94, B01D53/96, B01J23/38-468, F01M13-F01M2013, F02B47/08-10, F02D21/06-10, F02M26-F02M2026, G01M15/10, F02B47/06, F02D41, F02D43, F02D45, F02M3/02-055, F02M23, F02M25, F02M27, F02M31/02-186, F02M39-71, F02P5
	Air pollution abatement—Not elsewhere classified	B01D46, B01D47, B01D49, B01D50, B01D51, B03C3, F01N3, F01N5, F01N13, F01N9, F01N11, C10L10/02, C10L10/06
Water pollution abatement	Water and wastewater treatment	B63J4, C02F, C09K3/32, E03C1/12, E03F
	Fertilizers from wastewater	C05F7
	Oil spill and pollutant clean-up	E02B15/04-10, E02B2015/005, B63B35/32, C09K 3/32
Waste management	Solid waste collection	E01H15, B65F
	Material recovery, recycling and reuse	A23K10/26-28, A23K10/32-33, A23K10/37-38, A43B1/12, B03B9/06, B22F8, B29B7/66, B29B17, B30B9/32, B62D67, B65H73, B65D65/46, C03B1/02, C04B7/24-30, C04B11/26, C04B18/04-305, C04B33/132, C08J11, C09K11/01, C10M175, C22B7, C22B19/28-30, C22B25/06, D01G11, D21B1/08-10, D21B1/32, D21C5/02, D21H17/01, H01B 15/00, H01J 9/52, H01M 6/52, H01M 10/54
	Fertilizers from waste	C05F
	Incineration and energy recovery	C10L5/46-48, F23G5, F23G7
	Waste management—Not elsewhere classified	B09B, C10G1/10, A61L11, B02C19/0075
Others	Soil remediation	B09C
	Environmental monitoring	F01N11, G08B21/12-14

Source OECD, STI Microdata Lab: Intellectual Property Database, http://oe.cd/ipstats, created by the author https://stats.oecd.org/wbos/fileview2.aspx?IDFile=c5c477c0-d300-42fe-af1f-d4a450c79a39

$$\begin{aligned}\mathrm{PATENT_{WATER}} &= \frac{\mathrm{PATENT_{WATER}}}{\mathrm{PATENT_{POLLUTION}}} \times \frac{\mathrm{PATENT_{POLLUTION}}}{\mathrm{PATENT_{ENV}}} \\ &\times \frac{\mathrm{PATENT_{ENV}}}{\mathrm{PATENT_{TOTAL}}} \times \mathrm{PATENT_{TOTAL}} \\ &= \mathrm{PRIORITY} \times \mathrm{POLLUTION} \times \mathrm{ENVIRONMENT} \times \mathrm{SCALE}\end{aligned} \tag{5.1}$$

I consider the change in water pollution abatement technology patent applications from year t ($\mathrm{PATENT}^{t}_{WATER}$) to year $t + 1$ ($\mathrm{PATENT}^{t+1}_{WATER}$). Using Eq. (5.1), the change in water pollution abatement technology patent applications can be represented as follows.

$$\begin{aligned}\frac{\mathrm{PATENT}^{t+1}_{WATER}}{\mathrm{PATENT}^{t}_{WATER}} &= \frac{\mathrm{PRIORITY^{t+1}}}{\mathrm{PRIORITY^{t}}} \times \frac{\mathrm{POLLUTION^{t+1}}}{\mathrm{POLLUTION^{t}}} \\ &\times \frac{\mathrm{ENVIRONMENT^{t+1}}}{\mathrm{ENVIRONMENT^{t}}} \times \frac{\mathrm{SCALE^{t+1}}}{\mathrm{SCALE^{t}}}\end{aligned} \tag{5.2}$$

Equation (5.2) can be transformed into a natural logarithmic function and thus obtain Eq. (5.3).

$$\begin{aligned}\ln\left(\mathrm{PATENT}^{t+1}_{WATER}\right) - \ln\left(\mathrm{PATENT}^{t}_{WATER}\right) &= \ln\left(\frac{\mathrm{PRIORITY}^{t+1}}{\mathrm{PRIORITY}^{t}}\right) + \ln\left(\frac{\mathrm{POLLUTION}^{t+1}}{\mathrm{POLLUTION}^{t}}\right) \\ &+ \ln\left(\frac{\mathrm{ENVIRONMENT}^{t+1}}{\mathrm{ENVIRONMENT}^{t}}\right) + \ln\left(\frac{\mathrm{SCALE}^{t+1}}{\mathrm{SCALE}^{t}}\right)\end{aligned} \tag{5.3}$$

Multiplying both sides of Eq. (5.3) by $\omega_t^{t+1} = \left(\mathrm{PATENT}^{t+1}_{WATER} - \mathrm{PATENT}^{t}_{WATER}\right) / \left\{\ln\left(\mathrm{PATENT}^{t+1}_{WATER}\right) - \ln\left(\mathrm{PATENT}^{t}_{WATER}\right)\right\}$ yields Eq. (5.4):

$$\begin{aligned}\mathrm{PATENT}^{t+1}_{WATER} - \mathrm{PATENT}^{t}_{WATER} &= \Delta\mathrm{PATENT}^{t,t+1}_{WATER} \\ &= \omega_{\mathrm{t}}^{\mathrm{t+1}}\ln\left(\frac{\mathrm{PRIORITY^{t+1}}}{\mathrm{PRIORITY^{t}}}\right) + \omega_{\mathrm{t}}^{\mathrm{t+1}}\ln\left(\frac{\mathrm{POLLUTION^{t+1}}}{\mathrm{POLLUTION^{t}}}\right) \\ &+ \omega_{\mathrm{t}}^{\mathrm{t+1}}\ln\left(\frac{\mathrm{ENVIRONMENT^{t+1}}}{\mathrm{ENVIRONMENT^{t}}}\right) + \omega_{\mathrm{t}}^{\mathrm{t+1}}\ln\left(\frac{\mathrm{SCALE^{t+1}}}{\mathrm{SCALE^{t}}}\right)\end{aligned} \tag{5.4}$$

Therefore, changes in the number of patent applications for water pollution abatement technologies ($\Delta\mathrm{PATENT}^{t,t+1}_{WATER}$) are decomposed based on changes in PRIORITY (first term), POLLUTION (second term), ENVIRONMENT (third term), and SCALE (fourth term). The term ω_t^{t+1} operates as an additive weight to estimate the number of patents published for water pollution abatement technologies.

5.4 Comparative Analysis of Pollution Control Technology Patent Inventions

5.4.1 Comparative Analysis of IP5 Patent Invention Strategies

Comparative analysis across the five major patent offices (IP5) reveals important trends in global innovation patterns (see Table 5.2). China (CNIPA) emerged as the dominant player, with 765,186 applications from 1990 to 2022, significantly outpacing Japan (433,720), the United States (285,234), Korea (193,769), and Europe (165,370). This remarkable growth reflects China's strategic emphasis on environmental technology development as part of its economic transformation and environmental protection policies.

The technology mix varies significantly across offices, reflecting different environmental challenges and policy emphases. Water treatment technologies dominate Chinese applications (39%), addressing the country's critical water quality challenges arising from rapid industrialization. In contrast, air pollution control represents the largest share in the USPTO (55%), EPO (53%), and JPO (50%), reflecting different regulatory frameworks and industrial structures. The KIPO exhibits a relatively balanced portfolio, with air pollution control accounting for 40% and water pollution abatement for 34%, suggesting Korea's diversified approach to environmental technology development.

Figure 5.3 visualizes the evolution across all IP5 offices from 1990 to 2022, providing a comprehensive view of global innovation dynamics. China's patent filing

Table 5.2 Number of pollution control patent applications from 1990 to 2022

Patent office		Total	Air pollution abatement	Water pollution abatement	Waste management	Others
CNIPA	Patent	765,186	240,043	301,331	206,497	17,315
	Share	100%	31%	39%	27%	2%
USPTO	Patent	285,234	155,962	71,207	51,598	6467
	Share	100%	55%	25%	18%	2%
EPO	Patent	165,370	87,978	39,762	34,823	2807
	Share	100%	53%	24%	21%	2%
JPO	Patent	433,720	217,159	119,002	90,936	6623
	Share	100%	50%	27%	21%	2%
KIPO	Patent	193,769	77,672	65,065	48,027	3005
	Share	100%	40%	34%	25%	2%

Note Share represents the percentage of patent applications for each technology of total pollution control technology

Source OECD, STI Microdata Lab: Intellectual Property Database, http://oe.cd/ipstats, created by the author

trajectory in pollution control mirrors the broader cross-sectoral surge documented in the preceding chapters, but with domain-specific policy accelerators. The exponential growth beginning around 2005 was driven by sector-specific regulations, most notably the Air Pollution Prevention and Control Action Plan of 2013 and the Water Pollution Prevention and Control Action Plan ("Water Ten Plan") of 2015, which created urgent demand for technological solutions across multiple pollution domains simultaneously.

This divergence became particularly pronounced after 2009, when China surpassed all other offices in terms of annual applications, overtaking even the JPO, which had historically been the largest filing office. In the pollution control domain, this shift was particularly driven by the severity and visibility of China's environmental challenges—including the widely reported PM2.5 crises in major cities and widespread water contamination incidents—which generated both public pressure and policy urgency for technological solutions.

The visualization in the figure also reveals important cyclical patterns in developed economies. Consistent with the cross-sectoral pattern identified in Chaps. 3 and 4, the USPTO, EPO, JPO, and KIPO experienced peak filing periods around 2010–2013, followed by gradual decline. In the pollution control domain specifically, this trend is attributable not only to the common macroeconomic drivers discussed previously, but also to the maturation of established regulatory frameworks—such as the Clean Air Act in the United States and EU air quality directives—which reduced the marginal incentive for breakthrough innovation in well-established compliance technologies.

This decline is particularly notable in the JPO, where annual applications decreased from a peak of approximately 18,000 in 2000 to approximately 6000 in

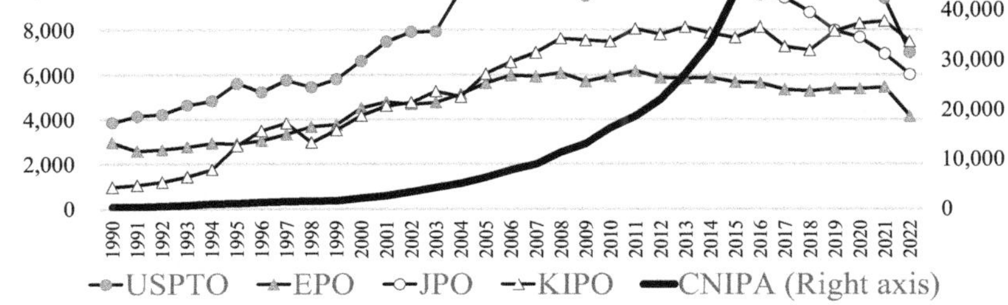

Fig. 5.3 Number of patent applications related to pollution control technology in IP5. *Note* While the 2022 figures in the current dataset show a nominal decline, this often reflects the conventional 18-month publication lag in patent filings rather than a reduction in actual R&D effort. *Source* OECD, STI Microdata Lab: Intellectual Property Database, http://oe.cd/ipstats, created by the author

2022, representing a decline of nearly two-thirds over two decades. This long-term contraction reflects Japan's demographic challenges, prolonged economic stagnation, and a shift toward incremental rather than breakthrough innovation. In contrast, the KIPO maintained relatively stable application volumes throughout the 2010s, with annual filings remaining between approximately 7000 and 8400, suggesting sustained policy support for environmental technology development in Korea.

5.4.2 Comparative Analysis of Technology Field Shares

Figure 5.4a presents absolute application numbers by technology field across the five major offices, revealing the scale and composition of innovation in each jurisdiction. The CNIPA's dominance extends across all categories, with a particularly strong representation in water treatment. Air pollution control represents the second largest CNIPA category, corresponding to well-publicized air quality challenges.

In contrast, the USPTO, EPO, and JPO show more balanced portfolios with a stronger emphasis on air pollution control. The USPTO applications are dominated by air technologies, reflecting the long history of Clean Air Act regulations and vehicle emission standards. The EPO shows a similar emphasis on air pollution technologies, driven by stringent EU air quality directives and automotive emission regulations. The relatively lower emphasis on water pollution in these two offices suggests either more mature technology domains or different regulatory priorities than in emerging economies.

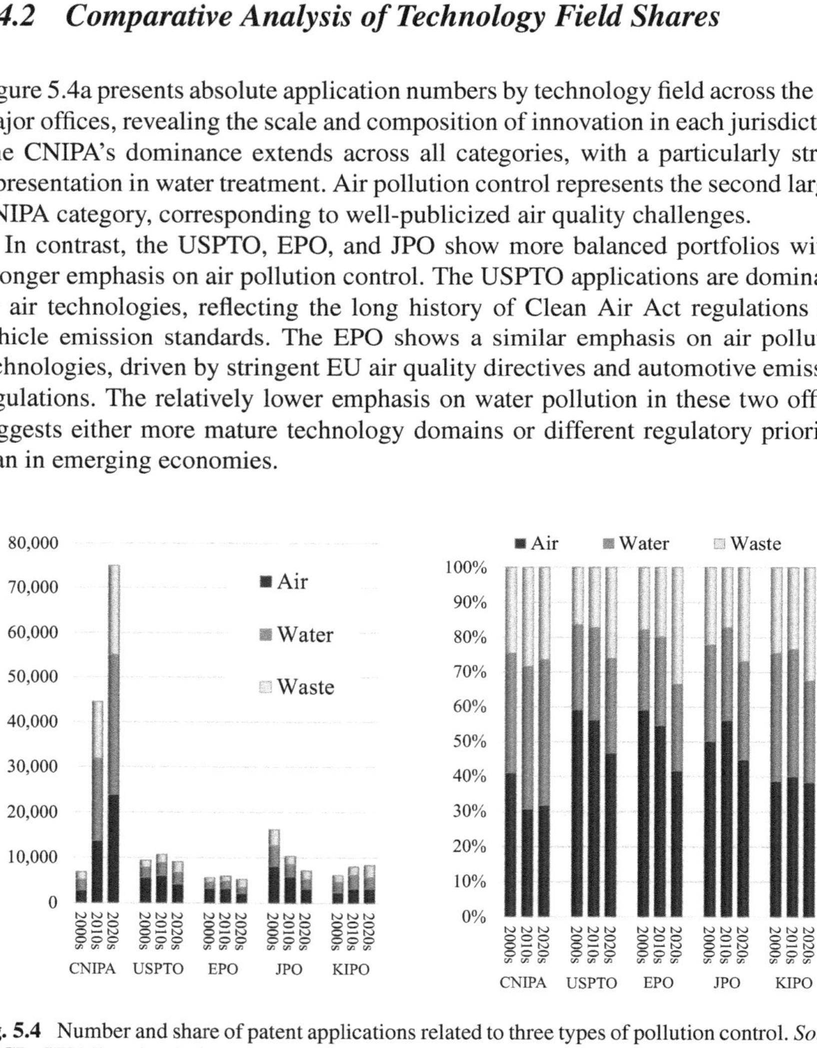

Fig. 5.4 Number and share of patent applications related to three types of pollution control. *Source* OECD, STI Microdata Lab: Intellectual Property Database, http://oe.cd/ipstats, created by the author

Figure 5.4b illustrates the relative share of each technology field within each office's portfolio, providing insights into strategic priorities and technological specialization. The figure reveals significant heterogeneity in technology composition.

The CNIPA's portfolio is dominated by water treatment (39%) and air pollution control (31%), which together account for 70% of all applications.

The USPTO, EPO, and JPO demonstrate different priority structures, with air pollution control accounting for 50–55% of the portfolios. This emphasis aligns with decades of stringent air quality regulations, particularly for vehicle emissions and industrial point sources. Water technologies constitute approximately 24–27%, whereas waste management represents 18–21%. The KIPO's intermediate pattern, with more balanced shares across air (40%), water (34%), and waste management (25%).

Analysis of decade-level trends reveals notable shifts in the technology composition of patent portfolios across the IP5 offices. In the CNIPA, average annual water treatment applications grew dramatically from approximately 2300 in the 2000s to 18,100 in the 2010s and further to 31,200 in the 2020s, consolidating water treatment's position as the dominant technology field. Air pollution applications followed a similar trajectory, rising from approximately 2800 in the 2000s to 23,800 in the 2020s, driven in large part by the Air Pollution Prevention and Control Action Plan implemented in 2013. Waste management applications also exhibited substantial growth, increasing from approximately 1700 in the 2000s to 19,900 in the 2020s, reflecting China's growing attention to solid waste and the circular economy.

In the developed-economy offices, a notable structural shift has been the rising relative importance of waste management technologies. In the EPO, average annual waste management applications surpassed water pollution applications, marking a reversal of the historical pattern where water technologies had held a larger share. This shift likely reflects the European Union's emphasis on the circular economy, as embodied in the EU Circular Economy Action Plan and the Waste Framework Directive, which have stimulated innovation in recycling, resource recovery, and waste reduction. A similar convergence is evident in the JPO, where average annual waste management applications approached parity with water pollution applications, and in the KIPO, where waste management applications surpassed water pollution applications in the 2020s. In the USPTO, waste management applications similarly converged with water pollution applications, while air pollution applications declined from approximately 6000 in the 2010s to approximately 4200, reflecting possible technology maturation in traditional air pollution control domains.

These temporal patterns suggest that while air pollution control has historically been the primary focus of innovation in developed economies, a gradual diversification toward waste management is underway, driven by circular economy policies and evolving environmental priorities. In contrast, China's innovation landscape continues to expand across all technology fields simultaneously, reflecting the country's need to address multiple severe environmental challenges concurrently.

5.5 Results of the Patent Decomposition Analysis

5.5.1 Results of the Patent Decomposition Analysis for the CNIPA

Figure 5.5 shows the CNIPA's remarkable patent growth from the 1990s to the 2020s, with particularly rapid increases from the 2000s through the 2010s, which is strongly related to the strengthening of environmental policies. During this period, the total number of pollution control patent applications increased substantially across all three subcategories—air pollution, water pollution, and waste management—as shown in the decomposition results.

The results of the decomposition analysis reveal three primary drivers of China's patent growth: the SCALE effect makes the largest contribution to the increase in the 2000s–2010s, reflecting the expansion of China's overall patent application activity driven by the institutional and policy incentives discussed in detail in Chap. 3 (Sect. 3.5.1). Pollution control technologies benefited substantially from this broader patent surge. In the 2010s–2020s, while the SCALE effect remained substantial, its relative dominance diminished as the ENVIRONMENT effect grew to comparable magnitude.

The ENVIRONMENT effect positively contributes to the increase in pollution control patent applications, which indicates that within China's overall patent portfolio, resource allocation to environmental technologies has increased. In the late 2000s, facing severe air and water pollution, China positioned environmental protection as a key priority in the 11th Five-Year Plan in 2006 (Schreifels et al., 2012). The successive announcement of the Air Pollution Prevention and Control Action Plan in 2013, Water Pollution Prevention and Control Action Plan in 2015, and Soil Pollution Prevention and Control Action Plan in 2016 significantly increased investment

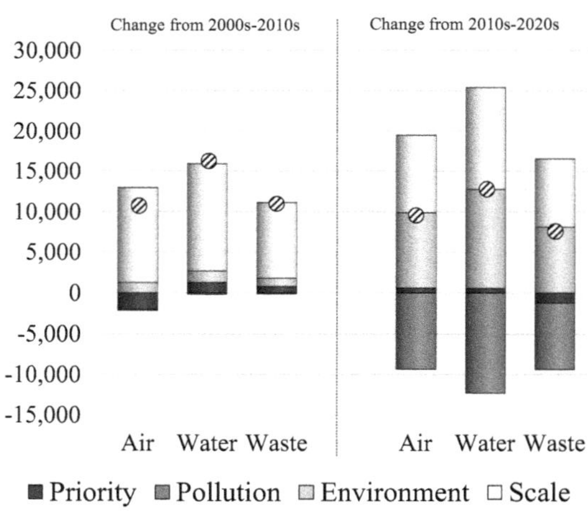

Fig. 5.5 Results of the patent decomposition analysis for the CNIPA. *Note* The y-axis is standardized such that the number of patent changes in the first year of each period is zero. The sum of the bars equals the value of the plotted points

in environmental technology development. The magnitude of the ENVIRONMENT effect increased dramatically from the 2000s–2010s to the 2010s–2020s. This sharp increase suggests that China's policy emphasis on environmental innovation intensified considerably during the 2010s, with environmental technologies commanding an increasingly larger share of total patent activity.

The POLLUTION indicator shows relatively small negative values in the 2000s–2010s, suggesting that the growth rates of patent applications for other environmental technologies and pollution control technologies were comparable at the CNIPA. However, the POLLUTION indicator shows significant negative values in the 2010s–2020s, indicating that the number of patent applications for other environmental technologies is increasing much more rapidly than that for pollution control technologies. With respect to other environmental technologies, the number of patent applications related to "manufacturing process efficiency improvements" and "climate change adaptation" rapidly increased in the 2020s, suggesting a relative decline in the share of pollution control among environmental technologies.

The PRIORITY effect is relatively small but variable across subcategories and periods. This finding indicates that the priorities within pollution prevention technologies are shifting. In the 2000s–2010s, the PRIORITY effect for air pollution was notably negative, while water pollution and waste management showed positive values, indicating that patent activity shifted away from air pollution toward water and waste during this period. In the 2010s–2020s, this pattern reversed: the PRIORITY effect for air pollution turned positive, water pollution remained positive, while waste management showed a significant negative value. This reversal suggests that priorities shifted from waste management toward air and water pollution countermeasures during the more recent period. This change reflects the diversification of environmental challenges and the evolution of policy responses.

Water pollution control accounted for approximately 39% of the applications from 1990 to 2022 (see Table 5.2), representing the largest share and reflecting the severity of water pollution issues accompanying rapid industrialization. This dominance is also reflected in the decomposition results, where water pollution consistently received the largest SCALE and ENVIRONMENT effects across both periods. Air pollution control also plays an important role, with particular development of flue gas desulfurization and denitrification technologies in response to PM2.5 problems in major metropolitan areas. The shift in PRIORITY toward air pollution in the 2010s–2020s aligns with China's heightened public awareness of air quality issues and the government's intensified regulatory efforts following the severe smog episodes in 2013.

5.5.2 Results of the Patent Decomposition Analysis for the USPTO

U.S. patents exhibit a development pattern that is different from that of China (Fig. 5.6). The United States already had a substantial filing base in the 1990s, achieved further growth in the 2000s, then peaked in the early 2010s and subsequently entered a declining trend. Specifically, the total change in patent applications was positive across all three subcategories in the 2000s–2010s, but diverged markedly in the 2010s–2020s, with air pollution and water pollution declining substantially while waste management was the only subcategory to register growth. The SCALE effect was positive in the 2000s-2010s but diminished dramatically in the 2010s–2020s, falling to near-zero levels, reflecting that overall filing activity entered a mature phase with slowing growth.

The ENVIRONMENT effect showed positive values in the 2000s–2010s with increasing resource allocation to environmental technologies, reflecting heightened climate change concerns and a clean technology investment boom from the early to mid-2000s. Notably, the ENVIRONMENT effect was the largest positive contributor to patent growth during this period, exceeding even the SCALE effect for all three subcategories. However, after the 2010s, the effect turned negative. As discussed in detail in Chap. 3 (Sect. 3.5.2), this reversal was driven by multiple factors, including the improved relative competitiveness of fossil fuels following the shale gas revolution, the decreased priority of climate change countermeasures during the Trump administration, and federal environmental deregulation.

For pollution control technologies specifically, the decline since the early 2010s also reflects domain-specific factors: the shale gas revolution promoted a shift from coal-fired to gas-fired power generation with lower environmental impact, thereby

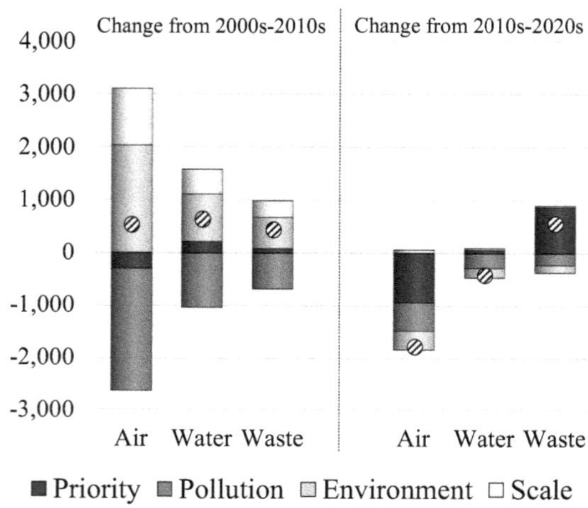

Fig. 5.6 Results of the patent decomposition analysis for the USPTO. *Note* The y-axis is standardized such that the number of patent changes in the first year of each period is zero. The sum of the bars equals the value of the plotted points

decreasing demand for certain pollution control technologies. Additionally, technology maturation in this field progressed, decreasing the opportunity for innovative development.

The POLLUTION indicator was substantially negative in both periods, suggesting that the patent application growth rate for pollution control technologies at the USPTO was low compared with that for other environmental technologies. In the 2000s–2010s, the POLLUTION effect was particularly large in magnitude for air pollution and water pollution, indicating that the divergence between pollution control and other environmental technologies was already pronounced during this period. In the 2010s–2020s, the POLLUTION effect remained negative but diminished considerably, suggesting that the gap in growth rates between pollution control and other environmental technologies narrowed somewhat. Among other environmental technologies at the USPTO during the 2010s, information and communication technologies such as "Energy efficient computing" and "Energy efficiency in communication networks," along with "Energy efficiency in buildings" and "Improvements in manufacturing process efficiency," experienced rapid growth. This finding suggests a decline in the relative share of pollution control technologies within the broader field of environmental technologies.

The PRIORITY indicator showed different trends for the 2000s–2010s and 2010s–2020s. In the 2000s–2010s, its contribution to total patent applications was relatively small, suggesting little difference in the growth rates of patent applications across the three subcategories. Conversely, in the 2010s–2020s, the PRIORITY indicator became the dominant driver of divergence among subcategories, indicating a significant shift in R&D priority from air pollution prevention technologies to waste management technologies. For air pollution, the PRIORITY effect accounted for approximately 53% of the total decline, while for waste management, the PRIORITY effect exceeded the total change, offsetting the negative contributions from the POLLUTION and ENVIRONMENT effects. One reason for the surge in waste management technology research in the U.S. during the 2020s is the substantial increase in the number of patent applications related to "Material recovery, recycling and reuse." This increase suggests that many companies advanced R&D in response to heightened technological demand for battery recovery and reuse, driven by the expanding market share of electric vehicles (the U.S. EV patent landscape is analyzed in detail in Chap. 4, Sect. 4.3.2).

5.5.3 Results of the Patent Decomposition Analysis for the EPO

Figure 5.7 shows that European patents demonstrate a development pattern similar to that of the United States but have distinctive characteristics. The number of patent applications showed remarkable growth in the 2000s, peaked in approximately 2010, and subsequently showed a gradual declining trend (see Fig. 5.3). The decomposition results confirm this overall trajectory: in the 2000s–2010s, water pollution and waste management registered modest growth, while air pollution experienced a slight decline. In the 2010s–2020s, the downturn became more pronounced, with air pollution and water pollution declining substantially, while waste management was the only subcategory to show growth.

The SCALE effect was positive from the 2000s to the 2010s, with the expansion of overall filing activity driven by economic expansion through EU enlargement and increased R&D investment based on the Lisbon Strategy. However, the 2008 global financial crisis and subsequent Eurozone debt crisis—whose impact on European patent activity and renewable energy investment is discussed in detail in Chap. 3 (Sect. 3.5.3)—diminished the SCALE effect substantially in the 2010s–2020s, though it remained positive. The continued, albeit much smaller, positive SCALE values indicate that overall European patent filing activity still expanded marginally even in the 2010s–2020s.

The ENVIRONMENT effect most prominently demonstrates European characteristics. It showed consistently positive values in the 2000s–2010s, indicating high resource allocation to environmental technologies. Notably, the ENVIRONMENT effect was the largest positive contributor to patent growth during this period, exceeding the SCALE effect for all three subcategories. This finding reflects Europe's strong policy commitment to environmental innovation through the comprehensive climate change framework—including the EU-ETS, the "20-20-20 targets," and renewable energy directives—discussed in Chap. 3 (Sect. 3.5.3; see also Ellerman & Buchner, 2008). However, in the 2010s–2020s, the ENVIRONMENT effect essentially vanished, falling to near-zero values. This dramatic shift suggests that the expansion of environmental technologies' share within overall patent portfolios reached a plateau. Unlike the USPTO, where the ENVIRONMENT effect

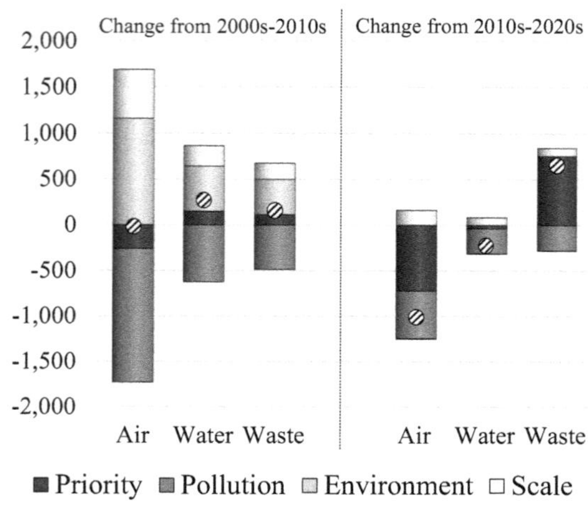

Fig. 5.7 Results of the patent decomposition analysis for the EPO. *Note* The y-axis is standardized such that the number of patent changes in the first year of each period is zero. The sum of the bars equals the value of the plotted points

turned clearly negative, the EPO's near-zero values indicate that Europe maintained its existing level of commitment to environmental innovation without further expansion—a pattern consistent with the institutional stability of the EU-ETS and continued regulatory frameworks.

The POLLUTION indicator was substantially negative in both periods, suggesting that the growth rate of patent applications for pollution control technologies at the EPO was lower than that of other environmental technologies. In the 2000s–2010s, the POLLUTION effect was strongly negative, indicating a significant divergence between pollution control and other environmental technology growth rates. In the 2010s–2020s, the POLLUTION values became less negative, suggesting that the growth rate gap between pollution control and other environmental technologies narrowed over time. This pattern parallels the trend observed at the USPTO. In other environmental technology fields at the EPO during the 2010s, "Energy-efficient computing," "Technologies related to metal processing," and "Technologies in the production process for final industrial or consumer products" experienced rapid growth. This finding suggests a relative decline in the share of pollution control technologies within the broader environmental technology sector.

The PRIORITY indicator of the EPO shows a trend broadly consistent with that of the USPTO. From the 2000s to the 2010s, the PRIORITY effect was modest in magnitude, indicating relatively limited shifts in subcategory composition. However, from the 2010s to the 2020s, the PRIORITY indicator became the dominant driver of divergence among subcategories, with air pollution showing a strongly negative value and waste management showing a large positive value. This finding indicates a significant shift in R&D focus from air pollution control technologies to waste management technologies. For air pollution, the PRIORITY effect accounted for approximately 67% of the total decline, while for waste management, the PRIORITY effect exceeded the total change, fully offsetting the negative contributions from the POLLUTION and ENVIRONMENT effects.

As noted in the analysis of the USPTO results, this shift can be attributed to increased demand for battery recovery and reuse technologies driven by the proliferation of electric vehicles (the European EV patent landscape is analyzed in detail in Chap. 4, Sect. 4.3.3). Furthermore, the promotion of R&D aimed at achieving a circular economy in Europe suggests a push for the research and development of waste management technologies focused on resource circulation. The European Commission's Circular Economy Action Plan, first adopted in 2015 and updated in 2020 as part of the European Green Deal, has provided a strong policy framework for this shift, explicitly targeting improvements in waste management, recycling technologies, and sustainable product design.

5.5.4 *Results of the Patent Decomposition Analysis for the JPO*

This section examines the patent factor decomposition for pollution control technology patents filed with the JPO. As shown in Fig. 5.8, Japanese pollution control technology patents, while showing patterns similar to those of other developed countries, have characteristics reflecting Japan's unique industrial structure and environmental policies. Unlike the USPTO and EPO, where some subcategories experienced growth in the 2000s–2010s, the JPO saw declines across all three subcategories during this period. In the 2010s–2020s, air pollution continued its steep decline and water pollution decreased more moderately, while waste management was the only subcategory to register positive growth.

The results of the patent factor decomposition analysis reveal that Japanese patent trends demonstrate the country's prolonged economic stagnation and maturation of environmental technologies. As discussed in Chaps. 3 and 4, the SCALE effect showed consistently negative values throughout both decomposition periods—a defining characteristic of the JPO analysis. Japan's overall patent filing activity contracted during the prolonged economic stagnation known as the "Lost Two Decades," as corporate R&D investment was suppressed. In particular, the decline in international competitiveness of the manufacturing industry and the relocation of research and development bases overseas led to a decrease in domestic patent applications. This persistently negative SCALE effect is a defining characteristic of the JPO analysis, distinguishing it sharply from the USPTO and EPO, where the SCALE effect remained positive in both periods.

Triggered by pollution problems in the 1970s, Japan pioneered the introduction of strict environmental regulations and developed excellent pollution control technologies. However, as a result, by the 2000s, technologies had already reached an

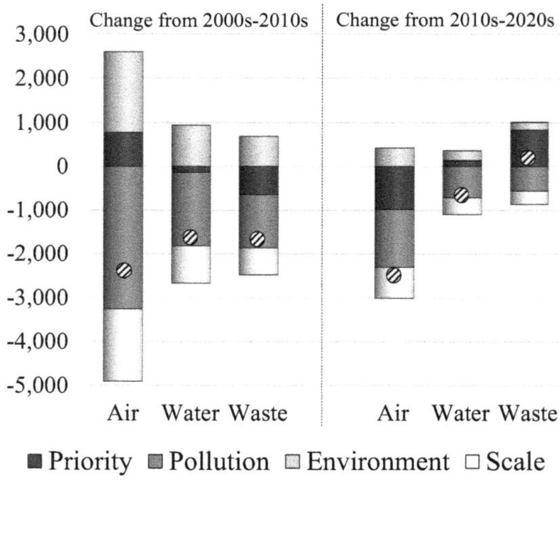

Fig. 5.8 Results of the patent decomposition analysis for the JPO. *Note* The y-axis is standardized such that the number of patent changes in the first year of each period is zero. The sum of the bars equals the value of the plotted points

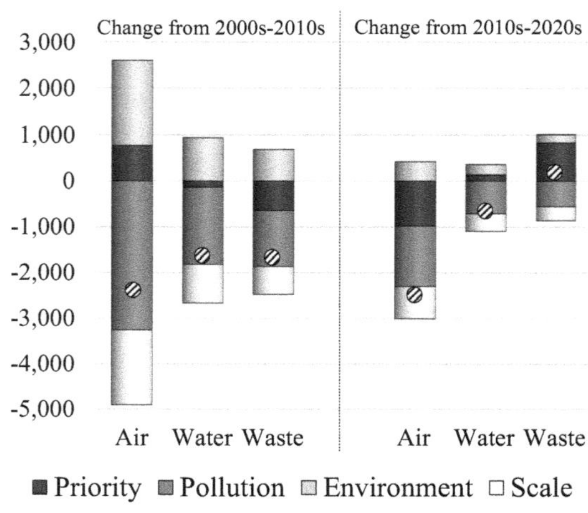

advanced stage of development and entered a mature phase. Consequently, opportunities for developing innovative new technologies were limited, with improvement and optimization of existing technologies becoming central. This situation has manifested as a declining trend in patent applications.

The ENVIRONMENT effect was strongly positive in the 2000s–2010s and remained positive but substantially reduced in the 2010s–2020s. In the 2000s–2010s, the ENVIRONMENT effect was the largest positive contributor to patent change and the only factor that partially offset the negative SCALE and POLLUTION effects. As the host country of the Kyoto Protocol, Japan emphasized climate change measures and expanded investment in environmental technologies in the 2000s. In particular, with the hosting of the 2008 Toyako Summit, Japan positioned its transition to a low-carbon society as a national strategy, and support for environmental technology development was strengthened. The magnitude of the ENVIRONMENT effect in the 2000s–2010s exceeded even the absolute value of the SCALE effect, underscoring the strength of Japan's policy-driven commitment to environmental innovation during this period. However, following the 2011 Great East Japan Earthquake and the Fukushima Daiichi nuclear accident—whose transformative impact on Japan's energy policy and renewable energy patent activity is discussed in detail in Chap. 3 (Sect. 3.5.4)—a review of the energy policy became necessary, and changes occurred in the priorities of environmental technology development. Importantly, unlike the USPTO (where the ENVIRONMENT effect turned clearly negative) and the EPO (where it fell to near-zero), the JPO's ENVIRONMENT effect remained meaningfully positive, suggesting that Japan maintained an expanding—though decelerating—commitment to environmental technology relative to overall patent activity.

The POLLUTION indicator was substantially negative in both periods, though the magnitude decreased from the 2000s–2010s to the 2010s–2020s. In the 2000s–2010s, the POLLUTION effect was the largest negative contributor to patent change, far exceeding the negative SCALE effect in magnitude. In the 2010s–2020s, the POLLUTION effect diminished considerably, though it remained the largest negative factor. This trend suggests that the growth rate of patent applications for pollution control technologies at the JPO was lower than that for other environmental technologies, though the gap in growth rates narrowed over time. This pattern is consistent with the trends observed at the USPTO and EPO. In other environmental technology fields at the JPO during the 2010s, an increase in patent applications was observed for technologies such as "electric vehicles" and "batteries." This finding is consistent with the results presented in Chap. 4. Additionally, technological development in manufacturing, such as "production process technologies for final industrial products and consumer goods" and "Technologies related to metal processing," experienced rapid growth.

The PRIORITY indicator of Japanese patent applications shows a notable reversal between the two periods. In the 2000s–2010s, the PRIORITY effect was strongly positive for air pollution but negative for water and waste, indicating that R&D priorities were shifting toward air pollution control and away from waste management during this earlier period. This pattern reversed dramatically in the 2010s–2020s, when the PRIORITY effect turned strongly negative for air pollution and strongly positive for waste management, with water pollution showing a small positive value. The 2010s–2020s pattern is consistent with the trends observed at the USPTO and EPO, indicating a broad international shift in R&D focus from air pollution control technologies to waste management technologies. For waste management, the positive PRIORITY effect was the primary driver of the subcategory's overall growth, fully offsetting the negative contributions from the POLLUTION, SCALE, and residual factors. As noted in the analysis of the USPTO and EPO results, this shift is thought to be driven by increased demand for battery recycling and reuse technologies spurred by the proliferation of electric vehicles. Japan's strong automotive industry and its early leadership in hybrid and electric vehicle technologies—whose patent dynamics are analyzed in Chap. 4 (Sect. 4.3.4)—may have further amplified this trend, as Japanese manufacturers actively pursued patents in battery-related recycling and material recovery.

5.5.5 Results of Patent Decomposition Analysis for the KIPO

This section examines the patent factor decomposition for pollution control technology patents filed with the KIPO. As shown in Fig. 5.9, Korean pollution control technology patents show an intermediate development pattern between that of developed and emerging countries. Korean patent applications steadily increased from the 1990s through the 2000s, peaked in approximately 2010, and subsequently showed a somewhat declining trend, but the degree of decline was not as pronounced as that in Japan, Europe, or the United States (see Fig. 5.3). The decomposition results support this characterization: in the 2000s–2010s, all three subcategories experienced growth. In the 2010s–2020s, the pattern diverged markedly, with air pollution registering near-zero change, water pollution declining substantially, and waste management showing strong growth. This mixed pattern in the 2010s–2020s contrasts with the USPTO and EPO, where air pollution experienced the steepest decline, and with the JPO, where all subcategories except waste declined.

The results of the patent factor decomposition analysis clearly demonstrate characteristics during Korea's transition period in economic development stages. The SCALE effect consistently showed positive values throughout both decomposition periods. As discussed in Chap. 3 (Sect. 3.5.5), Korea's aggressive R&D investment policy—with R&D expenditure as a percentage of GDP reaching one of the highest levels among OECD countries—drove a sustained expansion of overall patent filing activity. Major corporations such as Samsung, LG, and Hyundai Motor deployed aggressive patent strategies to improve international competitiveness. While the SCALE values declined somewhat from the first to the second period, they remained substantively positive—a pattern that distinguishes the KIPO from the JPO (where the SCALE effect was consistently negative) and from the USPTO and EPO (where the SCALE effect diminished to near-zero levels in the 2010s–2020s). Korea's continued positive SCALE effect reflects its ongoing trajectory of expanding R&D investment

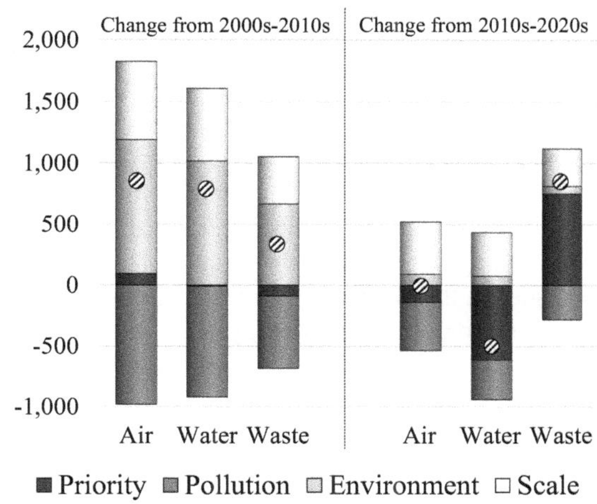

Fig. 5.9 Results of patent decomposition analysis for the KIPO. *Note* The y-axis is standardized such that the number of patent changes in the first year of each period is zero. The sum of the bars equals the value of the plotted points

and patent activity, even as other developed countries experienced stagnation or contraction.

The ENVIRONMENT effect reflects the evolution of Korean environmental policy. In the 2000s–2010s, the ENVIRONMENT effect was the largest positive contributor to patent growth across all three subcategories, exceeding even the SCALE effect. From the 1990s through the first half of the 2000s, Korea faced serious environmental pollution problems during its rapid industrialization process. Air pollution in major metropolitan areas, including Seoul, water pollution around industrial zones, and waste disposal problems have become social issues. In response, the government strengthened environmental regulations and expanded support for environmental technology development. During this period, the ENVIRONMENT effect was positive, with increasing resource allocation to environmental technologies.

In 2008, the Korean government adopted "Low Carbon Green Growth" as a national vision—whose impact on renewable energy patent activity is discussed in Chap. 3 (Sect. 3.5.5)—and promoted policies aimed at achieving both environmental protection and economic growth. This initiative led to expanded investment in pollution control technologies alongside renewable energy and energy conservation technologies. The ENVIRONMENT effect showed its largest positive values from the late 2000s to the early 2010s, clearly reflecting the impact of this policy. However, in the 2010s–2020s, the ENVIRONMENT effect declined dramatically to near-zero levels. This sharp reduction suggests that the expansion of environmental technologies' share within Korea's overall patent portfolio effectively plateaued. This pattern closely parallels the EPO, where the ENVIRONMENT effect also fell to near-zero in the 2010s–2020s, in contrast to the USPTO (where it turned clearly negative) and the JPO.

The POLLUTION indicator was substantially negative in both periods, though the magnitude decreased (became less negative) from the 2000s–2010s to the 2010s–2020s. In the 2000s–2010s, the POLLUTION effect was strongly negative, indicating a significant divergence between pollution control and other environmental technology growth rates. In the 2010s–2020s, the POLLUTION values diminished considerably, suggesting that the growth rate gap narrowed over time. This pattern is consistent with the trends observed at the other four patent offices. Overall, these results suggest that the growth rate of patent applications for pollution control technologies at the KIPO was lower than that for other environmental technologies. In other environmental technology fields at the KIPO during the 2010s, an increase in the number of patent applications was observed for technologies such as "electric vehicles" and "batteries." This trend aligns with that seen in the United States, Europe, and Japan. Furthermore, rapid growth in technological development has occurred across diverse fields, such as "Climate change mitigation in information and communication technologies," "Energy efficiency in buildings," and "Technologies relating to the processing of minerals".

The PRIORITY indicator at the KIPO shows distinct patterns across the two periods. In the 2000s–2010s, the PRIORITY effect was relatively small across all three subcategories, indicating limited shifts in subcategory composition during this period. In the 2010s–2020s, however, the PRIORITY indicator became the dominant driver of divergence among subcategories, with waste management showing a large positive value, water pollution showing a strongly negative value, and air pollution showing a moderately negative value. Notably, the KIPO's 2010s–2020s PRIORITY pattern differs from that of the USPTO, EPO, and JPO in one important respect: at those three offices, it was air pollution that showed the largest negative PRIORITY effect, whereas at the KIPO, it is water pollution that shows the most pronounced negative shift. This finding suggests that Korea's R&D reallocation in the 2010s–2020s involved a shift primarily from water pollution technologies—rather than air pollution technologies—toward waste management. For waste management, the PRIORITY effect was the primary driver of the subcategory's strong overall growth, complementing the positive contributions from the SCALE effect. As noted in the analysis of the USPTO and EPO results, this shift is likely driven by increased demand for battery recycling and reuse technologies, spurred by the proliferation of electric vehicles (the Korean EV patent landscape is analyzed in Chap. 4, Sect. 4.3.5). Korea's position as a major battery manufacturer—whose competitive advantage in this sector is discussed in Chap. 4—has likely amplified this trend, as leading firms actively pursue patents in battery recycling and material recovery technologies.

5.6 Conclusion

This chapter examines global pollution control technology patent trends across five major offices from 1990 to 2022 using the LMDI methodology to analyze drivers in air, water, and waste management technologies. The analysis first reveals a fundamental shift in the geography of innovation, with the CNIPA becoming the world's largest patent office for these technologies, reflecting China's dual focus on addressing environmental challenges and building indigenous capabilities. In contrast, developed economies like the US, Europe, and Japan saw filings peak around 2010–2012 before stabilizing, suggesting a transition toward incremental improvements in mature markets. Regional heterogeneity is further evidenced by technology priorities, as water pollution abatement dominates Chinese applications while air pollution control remains the primary focus in the US and Europe.

Second, the patent decomposition analysis shows that the four factors—SCALE, ENVIRONMENT, POLLUTION, and PRIORITY—reflect diverse economic and policy landscapes. While the SCALE effect drove growth in most regions during the 2000s, it diverged later, with China and Korea sustaining positive trends while the US and Europe stagnated and Japan faced persistent declines due to economic stagnation. The ENVIRONMENT effect varied significantly, strengthening in China after 2010 due to stringent regulations but turning negative in the US during the 2010s-2020s, likely due to the shale gas revolution and deregulation. Notably, the POLLUTION indicator was negative across all offices, indicating that pollution control technologies grew more slowly than other environmental sectors, such as electric vehicles and batteries.

Third, a significant shift in technology priorities emerged as R&D resources were systematically reallocated toward waste management technologies, particularly in developed nations and Korea. This trend is closely linked to the expansion of electric vehicle markets and the subsequent demand for battery recycling, reinforced by circular economy policy frameworks like the European Green Deal. These patterns suggest that pollution control innovation is entering a new phase integrated with transportation and energy storage sectors, moving away from traditional end-of-pipe solutions.

References

Albino, V., Ardito, L., Dangelico, R. M., & Messeni Petruzzelli, A. (2014). Understanding the development trends of low-carbon energy technologies: A patent analysis. *Applied Energy, 135*, 836–854.

Daim, T. U., Rueda, G., Martin, H., & Gerdsri, P. (2006). Forecasting emerging technologies: Use of bibliometrics and patent analysis. *Technological Forecasting and Social Change, 73*(8), 981–1012.

De Marchi, V. (2012). Environmental innovation and R&D cooperation: Empirical evidence from Spanish manufacturing firms. *Research Policy, 41*(3), 614–623.

Ellerman, A. D., & Buchner, B. K. (2008). Over-allocation or abatement? A preliminary analysis of the EU ETS based on the 2005–06 emissions data. *Environmental and Resource Economics, 41*(2), 267–287.

European Commission. (2019). *The European Green Deal. Communication from the Commission to the European Parliament, the European Council, the Council, the European Economic and Social Committee and the Committee of the Regions* (Report No. COM/2019/640 final). Brussels.

Ghisellini, P., Cialani, C., & Ulgiati, S. (2016). A review on circular economy: The expected transition to a balanced interplay of environmental and economic systems. *Journal of Cleaner Production, 114,* 11–32.

Johnstone, N., Haščič, I., & Popp, D. (2010). Renewable energy policies and technological innovation: Evidence based on patent counts. *Environmental and Resource Economics, 45*(1), 133–155.

Johnstone, N., Managi, S., Rodríguez, M. C., Haščič, I., Fujii, H., & Souchier, M. (2017). Environmental policy design, innovation and efficiency gains in electricity generation. *Energy Economics, 63,* 106–115.

Kim, J., & Lee, S. (2015). Patent databases for innovation studies: A comparative analysis of USPTO, EPO, JPO and KIPO. *Technological Forecasting and Social Change, 92,* 332–345.

Landrigan, P. J., et al. (2022). Pollution and health: A progress update. *The Lancet Planetary Health, 6*(6), e535–e547.

Lee, S., Yoon, B., & Park, Y. (2009). An approach to discovering new technology opportunities: Keyword-based patent map approach. *Technovation, 29*(6–7), 481–497.

Mao, G., Han, Y., Liu, X., Crittenden, J., Huang, N., & Ahmad, U. M. (2022). Technology status and trends of industrial wastewater treatment: A patent analysis. *Chemosphere, 288*(Pt 2), Article 132483.

Nesta, L., Vona, F., & Nicolli, F. (2014). Environmental policies, competition and innovation in renewable energy. *Journal of Environmental Economics and Management, 67*(3), 396–411.

OECD. (2024). Patents in environment-related technologies: Technology indicators. *OECD Environment Statistics (database).* https://doi.org/10.1787/e478bcd5-en

Popp, D. (2002). Induced innovation and energy prices. *American Economic Review, 92*(1), 160–180.

Popp, D. (2006). International innovation and diffusion of air pollution control technologies: The effects of NOX and SO2 regulation in the US, Japan, and Germany. *Journal of Environmental Economics and Management, 51*(1), 46–71.

Schreifels, J. J., Fu, Y., & Wilson, E. J. (2012). Sulfur dioxide control in China: Policy evolution during the 10th and 11th five-year plans and lessons for the future. *Energy Policy, 48,* 779–789.

Valero-Gil, J., & Scarpellini, S. (2024). Management of patented 'circular innovation' in view of the circular economy. *R&D Management, 54*(5), 1016–1039.

World Bank. (2013). *The economic costs of inadequate water supply and sanitation.* Water and Sanitation Program (WSP).

World Bank. (2016). *The cost of air pollution: Strengthening the economic case for action.* World Bank.

World Health Organization (WHO). (2021). *WHO Global Air Quality Guidelines: Particulate matter (PM2.5 and PM10), ozone, nitrogen dioxide, sulfur dioxide and carbon monoxide.* World Health Organization.

Chapter 6
Conclusion

6.1 Summary of Key Findings

This book systematically examines environmental technology innovation through patent data analysis across three critical domains: renewable energy (Chap. 3), environmentally friendly vehicles (Chap. 4), and pollution control (Chap. 5). By applying patent decomposition analysis based on the logarithmic mean Divisia index (LMDI) methodology (Ang, 2004, 2005; Fujii, 2016), the preceding chapters have elucidated the complex dynamics of environmental technology innovation across major economies and revealed the multifaceted factors driving technological progress toward sustainable development.

In Chap. 2, patent decomposition analysis was established as a useful methodological framework for understanding environmental technology innovation. The patent data provide several distinct advantages over alternative indicators such as R&D expenditure or academic publications (Haščič & Migotto, 2015). First, patents represent tangible outputs of innovation efforts, capturing technologies that have reached sufficient maturity for commercial protection. Second, the global harmonization of patent classification systems enables meaningful cross-country comparisons (WIPO, 2024). Third, the temporal and technological granularity of patent databases allows for detailed tracking of innovation trajectories and identification of technological convergence patterns (Fujii & Managi, 2019).

The application of LMDI decomposition analysis proved particularly valuable in disentangling the multiple factors influencing patent trends (Fujii, 2016; Fujii & Managi, 2017). This methodology successfully separated the effects of overall R&D scale expansion from strategic technological specialization, revealing that apparent declines in patent applications in specific domains often reflected rational resource reallocation rather than innovation stagnation. For instance, the decline in renewable energy patent applications in the 2010s–2020s was shown to result primarily from a strongly negative sector-specific effect (the RENEWABLE indicator, which captures the relative share of renewable energy patents within the broader portfolio

H. Fujii, *Key Drivers of Environmental Innovation*,
https://doi.org/10.1007/978-981-92-0060-3_6

of environmental technologies), indicating a sharp decrease in the relative priority of renewable energy within environmental technologies, rather than from a contraction of overall patent activity or environmental technology commitment (Kim & Cho, 2025; Nesta et al., 2014).

The analysis of renewable energy technology patents in Chap. 3 revealed significant shifts in clean energy R&D strategies. The surge in the number of renewable energy patents, particularly solar power technologies, observed between 2000s and 2010s indicates the impact of coordinated policy interventions. The American Recovery and Reinvestment Act, China's 4 trillion yuan stimulus plan (2008–2010) and the Strategic Emerging Industries policy, and European feed-in tariff schemes collectively created strong incentives for innovation, validating the induced innovation hypothesis that policy signals effectively direct R&D resources toward socially beneficial technologies (Johnstone et al., 2010; Popp, 2002). However, the subsequent decline in patent applications in the 2010s–2020s highlights the vulnerability of policy-dependent innovation to market volatility and regulatory uncertainty. The rapid reduction in feed-in tariffs across European countries, combined with falling fossil fuel prices after 2014, created challenging conditions for renewable energy innovation (del Río & Mir-Artigues, 2014; Wang & Krupnick, 2015).

The decomposition analysis revealed that the decline in renewable energy patents at the USPTO and EPO was driven primarily by the strongly negative RENEWABLE effect, rather than by a contraction of overall patent activity; the SCALE effect remained marginally positive in both regions. The ENVIRONMENT effect diverged markedly: it turned negative at the USPTO, reflecting decreased policy commitment during the first Trump administration (2017–2021) and the increased economic attractiveness of fossil fuels due to the shale gas revolution, whereas it remained essentially neutral at the EPO, consistent with Europe's sustained commitment to environmental technology through the European Green Deal and the strengthened EU-ETS. In China, the SCALE effect was the dominant driver from the 2000s to the 2010s, but a transition to a more strategic factor composition occurred from the 2010s to the 2020s, with the PRIORITY effect showing notable positive contributions for wind power technology, reflecting China's strategic positioning of offshore wind power as a key priority in achieving its "dual carbon targets." Japan exhibited a uniquely persistent negative SCALE effect across all periods, reflecting prolonged economic stagnation, while the 2011 Fukushima nuclear accident triggered strongly positive PRIORITY and RENEWABLE effects for solar power through the FIT system, though these gains were subsequently reversed in the 2010s–2020s as the domestic solar market saturated. South Korea maintained a consistently positive SCALE effect, contrasting with Japan, but shared similar patterns of negative RENEWABLE effects in the 2010s–2020s.

The analysis of environmentally friendly vehicle (EFV) technologies in Chap. 4 revealed the automotive industry's profound technological transition from internal combustion engine (ICEV) optimization to comprehensive electrification. In China, both ICEV and EV patents increased from the 2010s to the 2020s, driven by overwhelming SCALE and ENVIRONMENT effects. The PRIORITY effect showed a notable reversal: it turned positive for ICEV technology and negative for EV technology in the 2010s–2020s, reflecting a broadening of China's EFV strategy to include advanced internal combustion engines for plug-in hybrid vehicles alongside pure electric vehicles. It should be emphasized that this PRIORITY reversal reflects a relative reallocation within China's EFV technology portfolio rather than an absolute decline in EV patenting. Both ICEV and EV patent counts at the CNIPA continued to grow in absolute terms during this period; however, the share of advanced ICEV-related technologies, particularly those supporting plug-in hybrid electric vehicles (PHEVs), expanded relative to pure battery electric vehicle technologies. This pattern is consistent with the rapid commercialization of PHEVs by Chinese automakers such as BYD and Li Auto, which require sophisticated ICEV technology optimized for hybrid powertrain integration. In the United States and Europe, the PRIORITY effect was consistently negative for ICEV technology and positive for EV technology across both periods, demonstrating a clear and sustained strategic shift from ICEVs to EVs. This shift was particularly pronounced in Europe following the 2015 Volkswagen emissions scandal, which destroyed the credibility of "clean diesel" strategies and accelerated the transition to electrification.

Japan exhibited a distinctive pattern, with the SCALE effect being consistently negative across all periods and technologies—the only patent office among the IP5 to show this characteristic. The PRIORITY effect for EV technology weakened considerably from the 2000s–2010s to the 2010s–2020s, reflecting the "full lineup electrification strategy" adopted by Japanese automakers. South Korea, in contrast, demonstrated a "leapfrog strategy" of direct transition from ICEVs to battery electric vehicles, supported by its competitive advantage in battery manufacturing.

The analysis of pollution control technologies in Chap. 5 revealed distinct patterns compared with those of renewable energy and vehicle technologies. China's pollution control innovation grew dramatically, with the CNIPA recording 765,186 pollution control patent applications from 1990 to 2022, driven by both the SCALE effect and an intensifying ENVIRONMENT effect that grew to comparable magnitude by the 2010s–2020s. Distinct technology priorities emerged across regions: water pollution abatement dominated Chinese applications (39%), whereas air pollution control constituted the largest share at the USPTO (55%), EPO (53%), and JPO (50%), with the KIPO showing an intermediate pattern (air: 40%, water: 34%).

The decomposition analysis revealed that the SCALE effect at the USPTO and EPO diminished to near-zero levels in the 2010s–2020s, indicating stagnation rather than outright contraction. The KIPO's SCALE effect remained substantively positive, distinguishing Korea as an economy still in a growth phase of patent activity. The JPO stood as the sole office with persistently negative SCALE values in both periods, reflecting Japan's prolonged economic stagnation and the relocation of R&D activities overseas. The ENVIRONMENT effect exhibited the most varied cross-office patterns: it was strongly and increasingly positive at the CNIPA; clearly negative at the USPTO; near-zero at the EPO and KIPO; and meaningfully positive but declining at the JPO. The POLLUTION indicator—capturing the relative growth rate of pollution control versus other environmental technologies—was consistently negative across all five offices and both periods, indicating that pollution control technologies received a declining share of overall environmental innovation activity. Notably, the POLLUTION values became less negative from the 2000s–2010s to the 2010s–2020s across all offices, suggesting that the growth rate differential between pollution control and other environmental technologies narrowed over time.

The PRIORITY indicator revealed a systematic reallocation of R&D resources toward waste management technologies across all four non-Chinese offices in the 2010s–2020s, though the source of this reallocation differed: at the USPTO, EPO, and JPO, the shift came primarily at the expense of air pollution control, while at the KIPO, the most pronounced decline was in water pollution technologies. This shift is closely linked to the rapid expansion of electric vehicle markets and the consequent demand for battery recycling and reuse technologies, as well as circular economy policy frameworks, particularly the European Circular Economy Action Plan.

6.2 Cross-Chapter Synthesis and Methodological Contributions

Beyond the domain-specific findings, the parallel application of LMDI decomposition analysis across three environmental technology domains reveals several important cross-cutting patterns that would be invisible in any single-domain analysis.

The most striking cross-chapter finding is the persistent divergence in SCALE effects across patent offices, which proves remarkably consistent regardless of technology domain. The JPO exhibited negative SCALE effects across all three technology domains—renewable energy, environmentally friendly vehicles, and pollution control—and across all decomposition periods. This structural contraction of patent activity reflects macroeconomic factors (prolonged economic stagnation, demographic decline, and R&D offshoring) rather than domain-specific dynamics, as it manifests identically across technologies with fundamentally different market characteristics and policy environments. The CNIPA, by contrast, showed strongly positive SCALE effects across all domains, while the KIPO maintained positive values throughout. The USPTO and EPO occupied an intermediate position, with SCALE effects that were positive but declining toward near-zero levels. This cross-domain consistency validates the LMDI methodology's ability to separate structural economic factors from technology-specific strategic decisions.

The ENVIRONMENT effect tells a more nuanced story that varies by domain while maintaining certain cross-domain regularities. At the USPTO, the ENVIRONMENT effect turned negative across all three technology domains in the 2010s–2020s, suggesting a broad retreat from environmental technology prioritization that transcends any single sector. At the EPO, the ENVIRONMENT effect remained near-zero across domains, indicating that Europe maintained its existing commitment to environmental innovation without further expansion. At the JPO, the ENVIRONMENT effect remained positive across all three domains in both periods—a notable finding that distinguishes Japan from other developed economies and suggests that

Japan's challenge lies in overall R&D scale rather than environmental technology commitment. At the CNIPA, the consistently positive and strengthening ENVIRONMENT effect across all domains demonstrates the effectiveness of sustained policy commitment in driving environmental innovation.

A third cross-cutting pattern is the systematic reallocation of R&D priorities observable across domains. In renewable energy, the PRIORITY effect shows a shift from solar to wind power technology, particularly at the CNIPA and JPO. In vehicle technologies, a clear shift from ICEV to EV technology is evident at most offices. In pollution control, a shift from air and water pollution toward waste management technologies is observed. These parallel reallocations suggest that innovation systems across all five major economies are actively restructuring their environmental technology portfolios in response to evolving market opportunities, policy signals, and technology maturation patterns.

The methodological framework employed in this book makes several contributions to the field of environmental technology assessment. The systematic application of LMDI decomposition analysis provides a rigorous framework for identifying the distinct contributions of different factors to observed changes in patent activity. By decomposing patent number changes into technology-specific emphasis (PRIORITY), sector-specific indicators (RENEWABLE, VEHICLE, or POLLUTION), overall environmental technology emphasis (ENVIRONMENT), and total patent activity (SCALE), the analysis enables precise attribution of changes to specific strategic decisions versus broader trends. The comparative analysis across five major patent offices reveals patterns that would be invisible in narrower analyses. For instance, the consistent peak in developed economy patent activity in approximately 2010–2012 followed by decline, in contrast to China's sustained growth, suggests fundamentally different innovation dynamics driven by distinct stages of economic development and technology maturation.

6.3 Strategic Implications for Policy and Research

Advances in environmental technology represent both a critical challenge and a significant opportunity for humanity in this century. The transition to sustainable energy systems, clean transportation, and effective pollution control will determine whether I achieve climate stabilization, protect ecosystems, safeguard air and water quality, and sustain human well-being within the Earth's limits (UNEP, 2024). Promoting the development of environmental technologies complements changes in people's behaviors and consumption patterns and is an essential element for building a sustainable society.

This book has demonstrated that patent data analysis provides powerful tools for understanding environmental technology innovation dynamics. The findings reveal substantial innovation progress across all three domains while also highlighting persistent challenges, uneven development patterns, and the continuing need for effective policy interventions (Johnstone et al., 2010). Several key implications emerge for policy and research. First, the persistence of strong SCALE and ENVIRONMENT effects in China across all three technology domains demonstrates that targeted environmental policies can effectively stimulate innovation even in domains considered mature in developed economies. Second, the universally negative POLLUTION indicator in Chap. 5, combined with the strongly negative RENEWABLE effect in Chap. 3, suggests that both renewable energy and pollution control technologies are losing relative share within the broader environmental technology landscape as innovation increasingly shifts toward electric vehicle technologies, as evidenced in Chap. 4. While the present analysis does not directly examine battery technology or energy-efficient information and communication technologies, these adjacent domains likely absorb a substantial portion of the redirected R&D resources and warrant dedicated investigation in future work. Policymakers seeking to maintain innovation momentum in these foundational domains may need to consider dedicated support mechanisms. Third, the cross-domain shift in PRIORITY toward waste management and recycling technologies—evident in both the pollution control and vehicle technology analyses—highlights the emergence of circular economy principles as a unifying framework for next-generation environmental innovation. Fourth, the marked divergence in innovation volume and strategic priorities across the IP5 economies—particularly between China's sustained expansion and the stagnation or contraction observed in the United States, Europe, and Japan—underscores the importance of stable, long-term policy commitments in sustaining environmental technology innovation. The analysis demonstrates that market incentives alone are insufficient to maintain innovation momentum in domains such as renewable energy and pollution control, where regulatory signals have proven decisive in directing R&D resources. International coordination on environmental standards, patent harmonization, and collaborative R&D frameworks therefore represents a critical enabler for accelerating the global diffusion of environmental technologies.

Patent data analysis provides only one perspective for verifying innovation; however, it offers a valuable quantitative foundation for evidence-based policy formulation, strategic planning, and performance evaluation (Haščič & Migotto, 2015; OECD, 2024). With the expansion of patent databases, advances in analytical methods, and deeper integration with complementary data sources, patent analysis will continue to provide important insights into trends in environmental technology innovation. Future research should extend this analysis to examine the relationship between patent quality indicators and decomposition effects, the role of international technology collaboration in driving environmental innovation in emerging economies, and the integration of patent data with market deployment and diffusion indicators to provide a more complete picture of the environmental technology innovation lifecycle. This book has aimed to demonstrate the potential and future prospects of these analytical methods while acknowledging their limitations and the need for continuous methodological improvement.

6.4 Research Limitations and Future Directions

While this study provides comprehensive insights into R&D strategies using patent decomposition analysis, several limitations should be acknowledged. First, although patent data is a robust proxy for technological innovation, it does not capture all forms of innovation, such as tacit knowledge, organizational changes, or non-patented software developments. Second, the LMDI factor decomposition analysis identifies structural trends and correlations but does not strictly prove a causal relationship between specific policy interventions and technological shifts. Future research could employ econometric causal inference models, such as Difference-in-Differences, to further isolate the impact of specific environmental regulations on green patenting activities. Third, the apparent decline in patent application numbers observed in 2022 across all three technology domains should be interpreted with caution, as it likely reflects a data truncation artifact rather than a genuine contraction in innovative activity.

References

Ang, B. W. (2004). Decomposition analysis for policymaking in energy: Which is the preferred method? *Energy Policy, 32*(9), 1131–1139.

Ang, B. W. (2005). The LMDI approach to decomposition analysis: A practical guide. *Energy Policy, 33*(7), 867–871. https://doi.org/10.1016/j.enpol.2003.10.010/p

del Río, P., & Mir-Artigues, P. (2014). Combinations of support instruments for renewable electricity in Europe: A review. *Renewable and Sustainable Energy Reviews, 40,* 287–295.

Fujii, H. (2016). Decomposition analysis of green chemical technology inventions from 1971 to 2010 in Japan. *Journal of Cleaner Production, 112,* 4835–4843.

Fujii, H., & Managi, S. (2017). Decomposition analysis of water treatment technology patents. *Water, 9*(11), 860.

Fujii, H., & Managi, S. (2019). Decomposition analysis of sustainable green technology inventions in China. *Technological Forecasting and Social Change, 139,* 10–16.

Haščič, I., & Migotto, M. (2015). *Measuring environmental innovation using patent data* (OECD Environment Working Papers, No. 89). OECD Publishing.

Johnstone, N., Haščič, I., & Popp, D. (2010). Renewable energy policies and technological innovation: Evidence based on patent counts. *Environmental and Resource Economics, 45*(1), 133–155.

Kim, S., & Cho, K. (2025). Assessing international technological competitiveness in renewable energy: An IPC-based analysis of granted patents. *Sustainability, 17*(12), 5479.

Nesta, L., Vona, F., & Nicolli, F. (2014). Environmental policies, competition and innovation in renewable energy. *Journal of Environmental Economics and Management, 67*(3), 396–411.

OECD. (2024). *STI Micro-data Lab: Intellectual Property Database.* Retrieved November 25, 2025, from http://oe.cd/ipstats

Popp, D. (2002). Inducing innovation and energy prices. *American Economic Review, 92*(1), 160–180.

United Nations Environment Programme (UNEP). (2024). *Emissions Gap Report 2024: No more hot air … please!* UNEP, Nairobi. https://www.unep.org/resources/emissions-gap-report-2024. Accessed on February 17, 2026.

Wang, Z., & Krupnick, A. (2015). A retrospective review of shale gas development in the United States: What led to the boom? *Economics of Energy & Environmental Policy, 4*(1), 5–18.

World Intellectual Property Organization (WIPO). (2024). *WIPO patent database*. WIPO. https://www.wipo.int/patentscope/en/

Afterword

This book has traced the global innovation trajectory of environmental technologies by analyzing vast patent data spanning several decades. Analysis in each chapter highlights how technological development priorities shift dramatically based on market maturity, policy incentives, and each country's unique industrial structure.

In the renewable energy sector examined in Chap. 3, strategic priorities have shifted from the earlier phase centered on solar power generation to more advanced technological domains such as offshore wind power generation. Furthermore, in the environmentally friendly vehicles (EFV) sector covered in Chap. 4, while a clear and accelerating shift from internal combustion engine optimization to electric vehicles (EVs) became evident, strategic diversity was also observed. For instance, China is advancing internal combustion engine technology for applications in plug-in hybrid vehicles (PHEVs). In Chap. 5 on pollution control technologies, reflecting heightened interest in circular economies, prioritized investment in waste management and recycling technologies has become a global trend.

Particularly noteworthy is the "convergence" and "divergence" observed across regions throughout all chapters. While China achieves comprehensive technological growth backed by overwhelming "SCALE" expansion, Japan faces the structural challenge of overall patent volume contraction yet demonstrates a sustained positive ENVIRONMENT effect across all three technology domains, indicating continued commitment to environmental innovation despite overall R&D contraction. In the US and Europe, the data clearly show how changes in policy commitment—exemplified by the US retreat from environmental priorities during one administration and Europe's sustained commitment through the European Green Deal—directly influence resource allocation for environmental technologies.

The patent decomposition analysis presented in this book reveals that what appears to be a decline in patent counts often represents a rational and strategic reallocation of resources (a shift in PRIORITY). Technological innovation is not merely an accumulation of quantity but a process of 'selection and concentration' in response to the changing demands of society.

H. Fujii, *Key Drivers of Environmental Innovation*,
https://doi.org/10.1007/978-981-92-0060-3

Finally, I wish to express my deepest gratitude to the OECD STI Microdata Lab and other relevant institutions for providing the foundational data for this analysis. The intellectual stimulation provided by my colleagues and students has also been a major driving force in completing this book. The journey of environmental technology is still in its early stages; as an author, nothing would bring me greater joy than if this book contributes to the ongoing dialogue for building a sustainable society.

Most importantly, I would like to express my heartfelt appreciation to my family for their unwavering emotional support throughout all my research endeavors. I owe a special debt of gratitude to my wife, Yukiko, for her constant encouragement and patience, and to my sons, Kosuke and Yusuke, whose presence remains my greatest inspiration.

GPSR Compliance
The European Union's (EU) General Product Safety Regulation (GPSR) is a set of rules that requires consumer products to be safe and our obligations to ensure this.

If you have any concerns about our products, you can contact us on

ProductSafety@springernature.com

In case Publisher is established outside the EU, the EU authorized representative is:

Springer Nature Customer Service Center GmbH
Europaplatz 3
69115 Heidelberg, Germany

www.ingramcontent.com/pod-product-compliance
Ingram Content Group UK Ltd.
Pitfield, Milton Keynes, MK11 3LW, UK
UKHW021456050826
474026UK00003BB/7

* 9 7 8 9 8 1 9 2 0 0 5 9 7 *